The Country Club *of* Darien

The First Fifty Years

The Country Club
of Darien

The First Fifty Years

by Robert Lockwood Mills with contributions from Tucker M. Scott, Jr.

The Donning Company Publishers
184 Business Park Drive, Suite 206
Virginia Beach, VA 23462

Steve Mull, General Manager
Barbara Buchanan, Office Manager
Anne Cordray, Editor
Jolene Blevins, Graphic Designer
Derek Eley, Imaging Artist
Susan Adams, Project Research Coordinator
Tonya Hannink, Marketing Specialist
Pamela Engelhard, Marketing Advisor

Mary Taylor-Miller, Project Director

Library of Congress Cataloging-in-Publication Data

Mills, Robert Lockwood.
  The Country Club of Darien : the first fifty years / by Robert Mills with Tucker Scott.
      p. cm.
  ISBN 978-1-57864-491-9
 1. Country Club of Darien (Darien, Conn.)--History. 2. Country clubs--Connecticut--Darien--History. 3. Golf courses--Connecticut--Darien--History. 4. Darien (Conn.)--Social life and customs. I. Scott, Tucker. II. Title.
  HS2725.D282C686 2009
  367'.97469--dc22
              2009017345

Printed in the United States of America at Walsworth Publishing Company

Table of Contents

Acknowledgments

The author is indebted to long-time Country Club of Darien (CCD) member Tucker M. Scott, Jr., for assembling a huge archive of facts, anecdotes, and photographs. This is his book, in a very real sense.

Thanks are also due to former club managers Ken Koch and Bill Boulay, current manager Paul Kruzel, and members Tom McGrath and Tom McKiernan for their guidance. Also, to golf professional Ed Nicholson, his assistant Neil Lovelady, and caddy master Nick Holowiak for courtesies extended. Course Superintendent Tim O'Neill has been very helpful. The author also appreciates the generous recollections of Robert (Bobby) Stelben, Jr., and Dick Ettinger and is grateful to Phil Coviello, Paul Caswell, and Gloria Mullen for important background information.

At the Donning Company Publishers, Mary Taylor-Miller, Richard Horwege, and Anne Cordray have been stalwarts. Editorially, the author wishes to thank his good friend and fellow author Rosemary Strouse Clifton.

Various people submitted photos for use in the book, including Ashley Howell, Bernie Smith, and Al Palmer. Tucker Scott also gathered photos early in the writing process. The club would like to thank all those who contributed photos from their collections.

Introduction

The year 1957 was a long time ago in socio-economic and scientific terms, but not necessarily within the photographic memories of certain current members of the Country Club of Darien (CCD), who can still remember when it opened for business on June 29. On that date the Connecticut Turnpike had yet to open. The Merritt Parkway was only twenty-years-old and had a speed limit of 40 mph. The Throgs Neck Bridge hadn't been built yet. Nobody outside of Liverpool, England, had heard of the Beatles, and John F. Kennedy was still a U.S. Senator. The Cold War raged, but Vietnam was still being called Indo-China in 1957. Outer space was still outer space; nobody had gone there yet. It cost a nickel to ride a New York City subway train, and the Dodgers and Giants were still in town. Most TV sets in 1957 were black-and-white, and in parts of the United States blacks and whites went to different schools.

It's hard to imagine, but charter members of CCD were subject to no initiation fee and paid annual dues of around $200. The initial capital investment was $250,000...$1,000 per member. In 1958, when the eighteen-hole golf course was completed, a member inviting a guest on a weekday paid a greens fee of $4.00. A cold beer after the round cost $.75 at the bar; a perfectly stirred martini was $1.00. Caddies were not allowed to accept tips. Guests for tennis and paddle tennis paid $.50 during the week, $1.00 on weekends.

Times have changed. But it's fair to say the Country Club of Darien has changed less over the years than the world has. The golf course has been tweaked and toughened but retains most of what the original architect intended, and for all the improvements in golf equipment over the years, the course record of 64, set in 1959 by CCD's first pro, Mario Laureti, remains intact. The amateur course record of 67, since equaled but never bettered, was first set in 1980. Tennis is still tennis, swimming is still swimming, and on the social side, a well-made drink and a hearty dinner are no less enjoyable than they were fifty years ago.

This volume hopes to capture the spirit of CCD, which extends beyond the physical plant and even the prestige of belonging to it. CCD is about people, not things. It's unique in

that so many on its paid staff have been around for decades and still have no thought of leaving. Its members pay a lot more to join and in dues than charter members did, even adjusting for inflation, yet a huge percentage still give back to the club by serving on committees and otherwise helping out. This has been especially important since the members' takeover from founder Edgar Auchincloss in 1986; many routine tasks that theretofore had been taken for granted suddenly had to be assumed by volunteers.

This volume looks at CCD's first fifty years, from 1957–2007. Few of us will be around for the one hundredth anniversary history book of CCD in 2057. But we can imagine how its introduction might read, "For a century now our club has maintained a tradition of family togetherness, friendly competition, and social interaction. These remain our priorities for the next one hundred years."

CHAPTER
1

In the Beginning

Edgar S. Auchincloss had an idea. It was 1956 and "Keewaydin," a two hundred-plus-acre "gentleman's farm" in Darien, Connecticut, that his family had owned since 1905, had become expensive and unwieldy to manage. Edgar's widowed mother, Catherine Agnew Auchincloss, was along in years, and Edgar himself had begun a successful career in investment brokerage seven years earlier. The property, which had provided relief from the summer

The farmhouse, ca. 1955, was the centerpiece of the Auchincloss family farm, "Keewaydin," in Darien, Connecticut.

Edgar S. Auchincloss

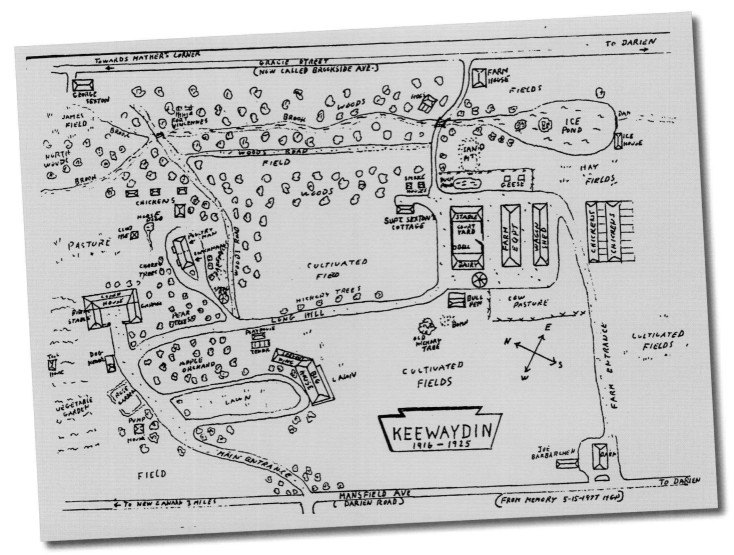

Apparently drawn freehand by Henry G. Pettitt from memory in 1977. Mr. Pettitt grew up at Keewaydin. His father at various times was a handyman, farmer, and chauffeur for the Auchincloss family from 1916–1925.

heat in the days before air conditioning, had become something of an anomaly in Darien, which by 1956 had evolved from a country getaway to an urban bedroom community for New York commuters.

Meanwhile, golf was undergoing its own bull market in the 1950s, owing to a confluence of factors. A post-World War II economic boom enabled an affluent leisure class to burgeon in the United States. Dwight D. "Ike" Eisenhower, the president almost everyone liked, was a golf addict whose every divot on the White House lawn drew media attention. And television, a post-war opiate for the masses, had begun to cover tournaments on a weekly basis, bringing into being a new kind of golf professional… one who played to the gallery, smiled for the camera, and signed autographs. The enormously popular Arnold Palmer, who first came to the attention of the golfing public in the late '50s, personified this metamorphosis, from an earlier era when wealthy golfers typically remained amateurs and struggling professionals (often former caddies) toured the country in relative anonymity, playing for meager purses before minuscule galleries. Almost overnight, golf's appeal crossed long-standing economic and demographic lines.

Edgar Auchincloss was a golfer himself. And he could see the short- and long-term potential if Keewaydin could be converted to a course. It was located conveniently on Mansfield Avenue, the major artery between the Merritt Parkway and downtown Darien, and along Brookside Road to the east, which connected New Canaan with the Boston Post Road.

The club's initial announcement in 1956.

Charter information.

Mrs. Catherine S. Auchincloss hits the inaugural shot in July 1957 as son and founder Edgar S. Auchincloss, Head Golf Professional Mario Laureti, and Golf Chairman Cliff Issacson look on.

Fashionable homes bordered the property on all sides, but it was clear none would need to be disturbed to allow a major reconfiguration. A club on this site would be geographically removed from established clubs in town (Wee Burn, Woodway, Tokeneke), and thus could more easily create its own identity.

The Auchincloss family didn't seek to relinquish title to the land, which they owned through the Keewaydin Corporation. Rather, in February 1956 a Board of Organizers, including Edgar and twenty neighbors, formulated a plan whereby 250 charter members would be solicited. Each would purchase a $1,000 bond (as capital for necessary renovations) and agree to pay dues according to their classes of membership for ongoing maintenance.

Dues would range from $325 per annum for a family membership with full privileges to as little as $100 for a twenty-one-year-old junior member. As an incentive to draw charter members, the initial 250 were promised 15 percent discounts on their annual dues. If and when this goal was attained, the Country Club of Darien would lease the property from Keewaydin Corporation under a non-cancelable twenty-year contract and could then begin operations.

Successful clubs with long waiting lists quite naturally create spillover demand for new clubs in the same vicinity. Darien was fertile territory. The other clubs were doing well, and Edgar Auchincloss's vision was quickly validated. By June 1957 the desired 250 charter members had been assembled, and the Country Club of Darien was in full operation.

CCD's first renovation project: the farmhouse becomes the clubhouse.

The CCD swimming pool as it looked in 1957.

As conceived by the Auchincloss family and the Board of Organizers, CCD was a country club, not a golf club. The distinction is clear. Golf reigns supreme, but tennis, swimming, and a busy social calendar satisfy a wider spectrum of interests within a family unit. Dad might be a golfer, while Mom prefers tennis. Their kids might grow up as future Olympic swimmers. A drink and/or lunch in the grillroom after golf might help close a business deal between a member and a guest; the dining room might bring the family together on the weekend. Parties, anniversaries, and wedding receptions would have familiar homes. In its earliest months CCD's charter members struck a balance; the golf course began as

The chicken coop on its way to becoming the pool bathhouse.

a nine-hole test in July 1957 (a second nine opened in July 1958), meanwhile money was found for a swimming pool (opened in 1958), six tennis courts (1957), and two platform (usually called "paddle") tennis courts (winter of 1958). CCD was immediately a country club with an emphasis on golf, as its founders intended.

Running a country club involves more than money and long-range planning. A Board of Governors was assembled, elected by the members, its primary mission being to organize committees to oversee each club activity. Meanwhile a Board of Directors was gathered to assume responsibility for the fiscal side, answerable at once to the membership and to Keewaydin Corporation, the club's landlord.

James J. Cochran, an advertising executive and charter member, was elected as the first chairman of the governing board. He had a formidable mandate and proved to be a wise choice. The club's membership had quickly expanded to 400 from the original 250; many were unknown to one another. If one imagines starting a business from scratch, hiring all new people to run it, and somehow growing the business and operating it smoothly at the same instant with a staff of relative strangers, one can appreciate the tact

The Auchincloss children's playhouse was destined to become the golf pro shop.

and management skill required of Mr. Cochran during CCD's early years.

On the building/development side, the club enlisted Alanmar Homes, a contractor in nearby Glenbrook, to construct a new clubhouse for under $80,000, based on a design by Page and Franklin, a local architectural firm. The cost represented just less than one-third of the original capital. The target date for completion was July 1, 1957.

Meanwhile other development evolved, not as new construction but as creative renovation of early buildings on the farm property. The original chicken coop became the bathhouse at the pool. The playhouse once used by Auchincloss children was redone into the first golf pro shop. Keewaydin's corn crib became the first tennis pro shop.

The golf course experienced its own evolution. Alfred Horace Tull (1897–1982), an English-born designer who had apprenticed under Devereux Emmet and had also constructed courses designed by Emmet, A. W. Tillinghast, and Walter Travis, was chosen to design CCD's layout. Tull had an excellent resume that included designs of Congressional Country Club in Bethesda, Maryland; two courses at Bethpage, New York State Park; duPont de Nemours Club in Wilmington, Delaware; Pelham, New York, Country Club; and nearby Country Club of New

The Halfway House.

Canaan. In 1969 Tull would re-design Westchester Country Club in Harrison, New York, improving on the original work of Walter Travis in 1919. Westchester Country Club was once regarded as one of the premier tests on the Professional Golf Association tour.

Tull's courses were known for ferocious bunkers and generous but difficult greens. He used water sparingly, and only to penalize truly poor shots. CCD's full eighteen holes were available for play in 1958. Edgar Auchincloss provided oversight and assistance to course design, as he knew the grounds so well from having wandered them since childhood. Even though CCD later underwent important changes, over time the imagination of Alfred H. Tull has retained credit for the vigorous challenge we confront fifty years later.

CHAPTER

2

A Club for All Seasons

The Country Club of Darien was off to a good start. By the summer of 1958, a challenging eighteen-hole golf course had opened for play, a swimming pool had been built, and six tennis courts were in use.

But the sudden changes in weather in the northeast corridor are ever present. From early November until the end of March, most outdoor sports in Connecticut are risky propositions at best, impossible at worst. Where golf is concerned, if the winter cold doesn't get you, the short hours of daylight will. So even before the second nine of the golf course had been readied for play, members were already taking up an outdoor sport conducive to cold weather…platform tennis.

Most platform tennis aficionados refer to their game as "paddle tennis." In point of fact the game of paddle tennis, which originated in Michigan in 1898, is quite different. It enjoyed most of its early twentieth-century play on the bare streets of New York, where raised platforms were and are impractical. Platform tennis, which utilizes paddles similarly but is played (most often in doubles competition) on an elevated surface enclosed by screening, had its genesis in nearby Scarsdale, New York, in 1928. The game's early momentum was stunted by the Great Depression and World War II, but by the time CCD opened it had become popular again, in particular among professional and amateur tennis players looking to keep sharp in the "off season." Bobby Riggs, far better known for his "Battle of the Sexes" tennis match with Billie Jean King in 1973 and earlier lawn tennis exploits, was in fact a platform tennis champion before ever picking up his first racket.

Play began at CCD in 1958. Cold weather has never had a noticeable effect on the enthusiasm of the players, who cheerfully don ski hats and gloves in even sub-freezing temperatures to compete.

Paddle tennis court.

The club further established its year-round bona fide entity by constructing a ballroom for social events, completed in 1959. A terrace was added the same year, adjoining the "19th Hole," always a popular year-round oasis for golfers and non-golfers. In 1960 flagstone was added on the terrace, and in 1962 a roof was added above it. The men's locker room was enlarged in 1960, a move of necessity given the rapid increase in membership.

CCD preparing for a match against Wee Burn. Top row, left to right: Bill Bohdan, Don Gorman, Paul Tuzinkiewicz, Mike Powell, and Carl Jaeger. Bottom row, left to right: Jim Hahn, Bob Lincoln, and John Corcoran. Courtesy of the CCD newsletter, Spring 2000 edition.

Left to right: Jim Millard, Bob Lincoln, Bill Bohdan, Tom Lom, Clyde White, Carl Jaeger, Ben Gifford, and Bob McGroarty. Courtesy of the CCD newsletter, December 2001 edition.

The Grand March of the Nutmeg Curling Club.

Chuck Owens, "Mr. Nutmeg."

In 1963 another winter sport, curling, cemented CCD's identification as a twelve-month athletic sanctuary. More than a few members had taken up the game (originally Scottish, and today the largest participatory sport in Canada) by joining the Nutmeg Curling Club, which was then based in Norwalk and utilized its overcrowded Crystal Rink.

Curling can roughly be described as akin to "shuffleboard on a long alley covered with ice." Competitors slide heavy stones along the ice, hoping to zero in on a target at the far end of the lane while dislodging any opponent's stone already occupying said target. Teammates may or may not "sweep" the ice as the stone skids along to reduce friction and keep it moving. Knowing when to sweep a stone is crucial to winning a "bonspiel."

Curling is an acquired taste. People tend to either find the game boring or are passionate about it. Most in the latter category are equally passionate about the customary bar activity that follows a bonspiel (match); in that respect curling and golf are two peas in the same recreational pod. Nutmeg Curling Club had something of a fraternity-house aspect from the start.

Margaret Mester at the keyboard.

Two early CCD members who loved to curl were Lawrence Achilles and Ted Bartlett. They approached Edgar Auchincloss, who also enjoyed the sport, with a proposition for a new rink on club property with construction costs jointly shared and with a rental commitment from Nutmeg going forward. Messrs. Achilles and Bartlett emphasized that the guaranteed bar revenue would be a tonic for the club's bottom line, especially since tonic water was typically accompanied by something more refreshing in the same glass at curling parties. New curlers, looking to stay active in the winter, immediately emerged from the golf and tennis crowds. In retrospect, it was an easy sale to make.

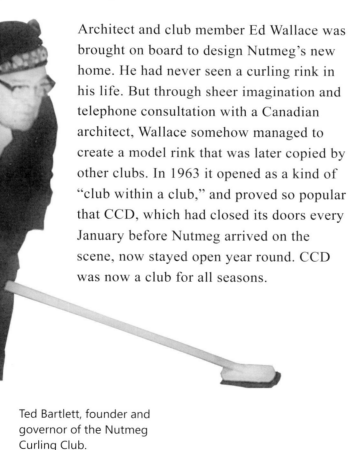

Architect and club member Ed Wallace was brought on board to design Nutmeg's new home. He had never seen a curling rink in his life. But through sheer imagination and telephone consultation with a Canadian architect, Wallace somehow managed to create a model rink that was later copied by other clubs. In 1963 it opened as a kind of "club within a club," and proved so popular that CCD, which had closed its doors every January before Nutmeg arrived on the scene, now stayed open year round. CCD was now a club for all seasons.

Ted Bartlett, founder and governor of the Nutmeg Curling Club.

CHAPTER
3

The Social Scene

The Country Club of Darien has always been a friendly place for members and guests. But no club can afford to take social intercourse for granted… left to their own devices golfers tend to mingle among themselves to discuss their sport, likewise tennis players and curlers. Over the years CCD has been proactive in developing "fun" activities that bridge the gap between disciplines.

Perhaps surprisingly, Edgar Auchincloss was skeptical at first about the club's social potential. Charter member Hugh Toumey quoted Edgar as saying in 1957, "There will never be a meal served (at the club)…." Edgar encouraged Hugh to look elsewhere in Darien if that were his preference, but Edgar's vision was too narrow in this instance. The founding members wanted a true country club and made sure the infrastructure kept pace with this goal. The ballroom was completed in 1959. In 1963 the lobby was altered, and in 1966 a new dining room was added. A mixed grill opened the same year and was modernized five years later. In 1988, two years after the members

Holidays are a special time at the club. Here the Easter Bunny visits with two youngsters. Courtesy of the CCD newsletter, May 2002 edition.

Mr. Romano, Mr. Mallozzi, and Mr. Siciliano at the annual Christmas Dinner Dance. Courtesy of the CCD newsletter, December 2001 edition.

acquired the club, the lobby, dining room, lounge, mixed grill, and ballroom were redecorated and the clubhouse entrance was altered.

When a member makes a hole-in-one or has an unprecedented round, typically only three other golfers are on hand to see it, and maybe two caddies. Rarely, if ever, does anyone capture photographic proof of an ace or a new course record. But memories of CCD's most joyous social events since 1957 do survive through numerous photographs, the common thread between them being that everyone seems to be smiling. Needless to say, smiles that accompany superb golf shots are typically counter-balanced by less than joyful reactions to wayward drives and missed putts in the same round. But everybody seems to birdie the 19th Hole at CCD.

Head Golf Professional Ed Nicholson has been with the club since 1976, a long tour of duty by any standard. Known for his professionalism, courtly manners, and steadfast encouragement of even the least skilled players

Ed and Sher Nicholson celebrate twenty years with CCD.

Bob Obernier, stage director for the 104th Kentucky Derby party.

Kentucky Derby party participants.

Clyde and June Craig at the 104th Kentucky Derby party.

Logan Miller calculating the CCD odds for the Kentucky Derby party.

to improve their games, Ed is now as much a fixture as the pro shop he runs. One of the many things that set Ed's pro shop apart from the ordinary is the annual Christmas party it sponsors every year for the members, a tradition that draws huge crowds of golfers and non-golfers alike. Ed's wife, Sher, provides a hearty buffet meal for the assembled masses.

Golf and horse racing share a betting element, and for three decades the signature event on CCD's social calendar was its Kentucky Derby party on the first Saturday in May. Members dressed up as jockeys and handled pari-mutuel wagering; mint juleps abounded, and for one day a year everyone was an honorary Kentucky colonel. For many "snowbird" members the occasion coincided with their return from second homes in the South. To the regret of many, the party hasn't been held since the mid-1990s due to scheduling conflicts, but sentiment seems to be strong for its reinstatement.

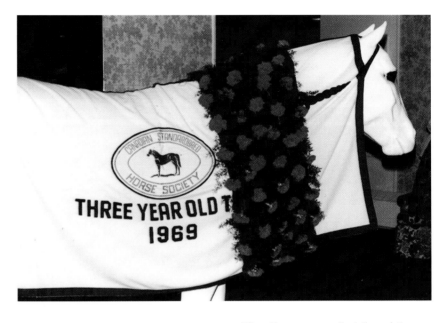

Clive Greaves supplied the white horse for the annual Kentucky Derby party.

Golf, tennis, paddle tennis, swimming, and (until 1998) curling have always created their own social frameworks in the form of dinners, luncheons, cocktail parties, even dances. But at CCD the golf and tennis crowds, in a kind of athletic cross-pollination, have often joined forces for all-day sessions combining tennis first, golf afterward, finally cocktails on the terrace. This is a boon to club harmony.

Over the years a dedicated cadre of members gravitated toward card tables in the clubhouse…most often, the men play gin rummy, the women bridge. The competitive gin rummy gang holds a tournament every year to crown a champion, who receives his honor at their annual dinner. Members of both sexes

Gin Rummy in the '80s. Far side, left to right: Tommy White, Tucker Scott, Tommy "Gin" McKiernan, Joe Romano, Phil Coviello. Near side, left to right: Bruce Beagley, Jim Murphy, Brian Clark, Dale Cunningham, Harry Dillon.

Gin Rummy in the '90s. Clockwise, starting at lower left: Tucker Scott, John McClutchy, Bill Whaley, Dave Ferm, Joe the bartender, Alex Noujaim, Doug Romano, Frank Anselmo, Brian Clark.

Gin Rummy in the modern era. Clockwise, starting at lower left: Bruce Beagley, Tucker Scott, Bill Whaley, Brian Clark, unidentified man, John McClutchy, Frank Anselmo, Joe Romano, Alex Noujaim, Tony Halsey, Bill San Fan Andre.

Gin Rummy players in the '70s celebrating Ray Irani's birthday. Front, left to right: Tucker Scott, Bruce Beagley, Fred Calve, Ray Irani, Lou Matusiak, and Jimmy Ippollito. Back, left to right: Tommy White, Logan Miller, Harry Dillon, Eddie O'Rourke, Bill San Fan Andre, John Gaughn, and Craig Hull.

also use the club's facilities to celebrate individual birthdays, retirements, and other special occasions.

The bridge group, whose history dates back to the founding of the club, assembles in the Ladies Lounge. Its growth has resulted in a spillover to the pub and dining room, which are used for frequent bridge luncheons.

All this social activity mandates that the club's service staff be both large and expert. Had Edgar Auchincloss's original skepticism not been overcome, CCD's dining facility could never have gained its oft-cited reputation as "...the finest restaurant in Fairfield County." As it is, the bar and dining room staffs are among the best qualified anywhere, with bartenders who stir an impeccable martini and chefs who own sheepskins from The Culinary Institute. These are paid employees of the club, of course...but in the country club spirit they find plenty of time to socialize among themselves. It's no accident that CCD's service personnel are known for both expertise and longevity on the job.

The ladies' bridge group in 2002. Seated, left to right: Sue Ceresa, Sue Holland, Pat Scala. Standing, left to right: Diane Gilliam, Sonia Smith, Harriette Meagher, Kathleen Lee.

OUR GOLF PROFESSIONALS
by Tucker Scott, Jr.

MARIO LAURETI 1957–1970

Mario came to CCD from his position as assistant professional at Scarsdale Country Club. An excellent golfer, his 64 in 1959 stands to this day as the professional course record at the club.

Dave Marr, on the PGA Tour for many years, was one of Mario's protégés. A practical joker, Laureti frequently came up with quips about the game of golf with an amusing smile causing his eyes to squint almost to a close. Some never knew whether he was serious or trying to be witty.

Mario is the originator of the phrase "Mr. A.," when referring to the founder, Edgar Auchincloss, and from then on, all the employees addressed Edgar Auchincloss as "Mr. A." until his death forty years later.

Nick Holowiak, assistant caddie master with Clark Collins, golf pro and Vinnie Adams, caddie master.

CLARK COLLINS 1970–1976

Clark grew up at the Mahopac Golf Club in Westchester County where his father was greenskeeper and head golf professional. Mahopac had a curling club and performed this sport on natural Lake Mahopac. Clark noticed CCD's superb curling facility and told this story himself.

As a kid, he thought he was playing a prank on the curlers when he discovered sixteen, forty-two pound curling stones hidden in the woods near the lake. He placed them in a rowboat and tossed them overboard in the center of the lake. They were never recovered. He told that at that time, he did not realize that this frivolous act cost the fledgling club over one thousand dollars!

Clark got the "Florida bug" and moved to Stuart to open a bait and tackle shop, giving golf lessons as a sideline.

1965 Junior Girls' Golf Champion Mary Lou Brameier at age fourteen (left) with Mario Laureti, golf pro.

ED NICHOLSON 1976–PRESENT

After graduation from Ohio State in 1964, Ed joined Lennox Industries in Columbus where he spent five years in sales. His business acumen was equaled only by this yearning to become a golf professional. Ed's dream came true when he became assistant golf professional at Scarsdale Golf Club from 1970 to 1974. From there, he became the head pro at Wykagyl Country Club in New Rochelle for two years. CCD beckoned and on December 1, 1976, he joined as head professional. From Wykagyl, he brought his assistant, Neil Lovelady, who has been a loyal member of his staff. The team of Ed and Neil form a nucleus of expanding operations through the past thirty years.

One of Ed's creations is the Pro Am Series during the season. An early sign up is a must, due to this event's popularity. Each team consists of three members with a pro, Ed, or one of his assistant pros, who play from scratch and the members with full handicap. The lowest net score at year's end becomes the winner.

With the new and larger pro shop, Ed's staff includes two or three other assistant pros. Daughter Amy was a real part of the operation when home from the University of Vermont.

The club acknowledges the hard work over the past thirty years by Ed Nicholson. Courtesy of CCD newsletter, July 2006 edition.

Today she resides in Boston with her husband. Wife Sher has been known to pinch hit when things get hectic. Caddie Master Nick Holowiak, just next door, is always on hand to help. Ed's well-appointed pro shop is stocked judiciously with clothing and equipment par excellence!

Ed's hard work and love for the sport has merited several awards. In 2002, he was chosen as the Merchandising Pro of the Year (private course category) of the Metropolitan PGA Association. In the year of the club's fiftieth anniversary, Ed was selected as the 2007 Professional of the Year by the Metropolitan PGA of America. This award is that association's highest honor and reflects a life of dedicated service and commitment to the game of golf and the PGA.

Assistant Pro Neil Lovelady with group of young golfers.

CHAPTER
4

Interesting People

The Country Club of Darien is more than the sum of its parts. A championship golf course is a great place to start. Tennis courts, a swimming pool, and comfortable rooms for socializing are important. Ultimately, however, a club's success is measured by the sacrifices of those who cherish it, especially when those same people bring extraordinary skills to the table.

Fred Calve, a decorated veteran of World War II and the Korean conflict, was a charter member of the club. He knew golf from having caddied at nearby Wee Burn as a boy and was already experienced as a landscaper by 1956. Before any building went up, in fact before the club was organized, Fred and his brother George contributed their expertise and equipment to the task of converting farmland into a golf course, a Herculean effort.

Ed Wallace, a charter member and an architect by profession, had never seen a curling rink in his life when he volunteered to design Nutmeg's facility at the club; it would become only the second in the state of Connecticut, the other being in far-off Norfolk, near the Massachusetts line. With guidance only from a long-distance telephone consultation with a fellow architect in Canada (where curling is almost a religion), Wallace produced a magnificent rink that Ardsley (New York) Country Club later copied to the letter for its own usage.

Vernon Burnham was CCD's first course superintendent. His history with the club extended back to when the Auchincloss family still operated Keewaydin Farm. Burnham happened to be seeking the vacant job of dairyman on the farm, so one night he boldly knocked on the Auchincloss's door to apply personally. In a later era Burnham might have been arrested as a trespasser, but Mrs. Patti Auchincloss was so impressed with his pleasant manner that she mockingly threatened Edgar with divorce if Burnham wasn't hired. Years later, not entirely in keeping with his duties as course superintendent, Vernon

went out at night to clandestinely honor the wishes of deceased founding board member Gerald Keyser, who had asked that his ashes be buried on the 7th Hole. This was a well-kept secret for many years.

Tim O'Neill has been course superintendent since 1981. He's now as much a fixture at CCD as the clubhouse and golf shop, but when he first interviewed for the job with Edgar Auchincloss, Tim was only twenty-two. Everyone at the club was older than he, so to strengthen his case for employment Tim grew a mustache. After thanking Mr. A. for the interview, Tim added that he'd like to "talk turf" at a subsequent meeting. To this day it isn't clear

Legendary Arnold Palmer tells Course Superintendent Vernon Burnham, "...I still have that 1930s tractor my father used to mow the fairways at Latrobe...used it in the Pennzoil TV commercials..."

Tim O'Neill, golf course superintendent. Courtesy of photographer, Larry Lambrecht.

whether it was the long-lost mustache or Tim's confident chatter about agronomy that got him the job, but everyone at CCD is happy with the way things turned out.

Mario Laureti, the club's first professional, came to CCD in 1957 from the prestigious Scarsdale (New York) Golf Club. Two years later he burned up the course with a 64, which still stands as the professional course record. Byron Nelson always said it's ungracious of a visiting pro to break any course record held by the local man, but it's doubtful if Lord Byron could have done better than a 64 had he wanted to. Laureti was a splendid player and teacher, but might have been better known for his practical jokes, wit, and trick shot artistry on the golf course and billiard table. Mario would wager he could get down in three shots on the 9th Hole from inside the pro shop, using a five iron and hitting through an open window. CCD's members quickly learned never to take him up on the bet.

Steve Zangrillo, a prominent Darien businessman, was a founding member and is patriarch of a remarkable family of athletes, all devoted members of the club. Steve himself was CCD's first champion in 1957 and won again in 1962. He holds the distinction of once having driven the green on Hole 2, a 357-yard par-4. In 1998 Steve's son Tony, who had won the junior boys' championship three times, won the

Left to right: 1968 Junior Girls' Runner-Up Sue Madden, Golf Pro Mario Laureti, and Champion Martha Scott.

club championship. Tony was elected president of the club in 2002. Meanwhile Steve's versatile wife Yolanda won the ladies' championship in 1984, having been tennis champion in 1968 and 1972 and platform tennis champion in 1969, 1975, 1978, 1980, 1981, and 1982. Daughter Gina won the junior girls' golf championship in 1975.

If such a person as "Mr. Country Club of Darien" exists, it would be Tucker M. Scott, Jr., whose catalog of memorabilia and anecdotes forms the foundation block of this volume. He was senior men's golf champion in 1993, but his involvement with the club has been so total, from the club's earliest years, as to render any single accomplishment relatively trivial. Ten years ago he began to assemble data toward the goal of honoring the club's fiftieth anniversary, an effort that has continued almost to the present.

Tucker Scott, Jr.

CHAPTER
5

The Lighter Side:
Humorous Moments from the Past

The past fifty years at CCD have seen major changes in the physical plant, improvements to the golf course, visits from golf immortals and other celebrities, the acquisition of the club by the membership, and hundreds of celebrations and social events of one variety or another. But when veteran members gather in the dining room or grill room over a drink, as often as not the conversation drifts to funny people and amusing happenings over the years. Tucker Scott deserves all credit and high praise for gathering a rich archive of such memories.

At one time the club had a dozen or so young members who styled themselves as "The Rat Pack," in the fashion of Frank Sinatra and friends of the live-and-let-live, post-Camelot era. Old Blue Eyes' counterpart as leader of the CCD Rat Pack was Ed Callahan. One summer night while a formal dance was underway, Ed and his pals, all a drink or two over the legal limit and seeking relief from the heat and humidity, left their black ties and cummerbunds in the men's locker room and plunged into the pool in their birthday suits. Nobody seemed to notice. After a refreshing dip, The Rat Pack all went back inside to dress, only to discover that a renegade member of the group had purloined their tuxedos…but only momentarily, after which the erstwhile skinny-dippers returned to the dance floor. Their wives, perhaps jaded from prior experience, seemed not to have known they'd been missing.

Long-time members recall a popular waitress who had a problem with counting. She always returned to the table with exactly one more drink than had been ordered…never two more, never one less. As the night went on and she repeated the same error, her speech would become slurred. Her loyal customers finally caught on that instead of returning the extra glass to the bartender, she'd always finish the drink herself. But nobody can recall an instance where she failed to show up for work the next night.

One fine day some fifteen years ago members Bob Russell and Win Watson discovered a new meaning for "birdie" on the golf course. It seems Win, who loved wearing Bavarian-style hats with protruding feathers, was strolling toward his ball near the 16th Green following his third shot. Overhead loomed a band of hawks, hoping to make a meal of an itinerant rodent or wounded bird on the ground. As he lined up his fourth shot, Watson heard a screech…one of the hawks had mistaken his plumed hat for something to eat and plucked it from his scalp before he could react. The story has a happy ending. The hawk quickly dropped the hat; Win put it back in place and, nonplussed, promptly pitched in for his second "birdie" on the same hole.

Stories of players with short fuses abound in golf lore. Bill Mikolazy is well remembered for driving three successive balls into the water on Hole 6 one afternoon about forty years ago. Rather than waste another new ball for his seventh shot, Mikolazy took his clubs and bag from the caddy and hurled the entire ensemble into the lake, not sure if the clubs or the lake was to blame for his misfortune but punishing both at once to play safe. Bill then repaired to the locker room, donned bathing trunks he kept there for just such an occasion, dove into the lake and retrieved everything.

Bonspiel with bagpipes and drums.

Marianne Fahey and Kay Reilly were enjoying a friendly match some years back when Marianne, at the wheel of their golf cart and in a state of reverie after birdieing the 8th Hole, drove the cart forthwith into the water hazard on Hole 9. After being rescued by Club Manager Jim Hutchinson, Marianne and Kay (according to popular legend) took advantage of the incident to replenish their golf wardrobe at the pro shop. Marianne's husband Bart wasn't amused; kidded by Edgar Auchincloss that the family might be charged for harming club equipment, Bart said he'd counter-sue because said equipment was faulty.

The Nutmeg Curling Club, with its active bar scene and members' predilection for post-match celebrating, provided many memorable anecdotes. Passionate curler Bert Blake (the present writer's late father-in-law), who was always among Nutmeg's most eager celebrants, is remembered for one incident in particular. It seems that before its present electronic system was installed, CCD employed a night watchman for security. Bert had alerted him to frequent odd noises emanating from the overhead loft. One night the sentry climbed a ladder to investigate, flashlight and loaded pistol in hand, as Bert nodded in approval of the strategy. "It's a family of raccoons; what should I do?" the sentry cried from above. "Shoot!" replied Bert. The watchman dutifully emptied his revolver at the critters; alas, every shot missed. It isn't known if this comical occurrence led directly to the electronic system's installation, or if it was merely a coincidence. In any event, the raccoons weren't heard from again.

Edgar Auchincloss was an avid curler, and one Sunday morning after his team had lost a match he accepted a Scotch highball from a victorious opponent according to the "winners buy" custom. Just then his elderly mother, a devout Presbyterian with a rather different notion of how to spend Sunday mornings, appeared at the staircase to the rink. "Hide this," Edgar whispered, as he handed his drink to a friend and moved to help his mother down the stairs. "No thank you," replied Mrs. A., who harbored no illusions about what had been going on. "I'm perfectly able to come down by myself."

Not everyone who over-imbibes at CCD pays a penalty. One night "Eddie" drove home from the club after downing a couple too many, having brusquely rebuffed offers from several friends who'd wanted to play designated driver. En route home Eddie was stopped by a patrolman who had seen him swerving about the road; just then another car almost struck the officer as it tried to pass, so it was stopped, also. As the policeman questioned the second driver, Eddie climbed into the idle patrol car, drove home and went to bed without a word to his wife.

Soon the officer, driving Eddie's car, arrived at the door to speak to Eddie, who had fallen asleep under the weight of accumulated cocktails. Seeing his own vehicle parked in the garage, the cop decided discretion was the better part of valor. He chose not to upset his chief by reporting the incident and possibly damaging his own career. Eddie slept on until the morning.

No chapter about humor would be complete without affectionate mention of Charles Mullen (1927–2002), the author's good friend and subject of *The Last Renaissance Man*, published in 2001. Lunch would often be at the club together, ostensibly to talk business. Inevitably the conversation would detour to a riff on public figures, show business, or historical oddities. Charles (occasionally Charlie, never Chuck) was no golfer, albeit Ed Nicholson once said he could make him one. In plain truth, wife Gloria and children, Claudia and Geoff, were the athletes in the family. Charles was unapologetically a non-athlete who preferred the 19th Hole; sports-wise, he might be best remembered at CCD for having invented something he called the "Auchincloss twist," a free-wheeling, non-Olympic-style belly flop from the pool's diving board into the water, occasionally while in full evening dress and always while fully lubricated. Charles's unfailing bonhomie, his talent for dialects and joke telling, and his bottomless reservoir of anecdotes from a kaleidoscopic life in show business and the corporate world made him a favorite of everyone. Charles Mullen, a CCD member from 1969 until his death, was indeed the last Renaissance man.

New York City former mayor, Rudy Giuliani (center) with Cindy and Tony Princi who hosted a fundraiser for Giuliani in March 2000.

CHAPTER
6

Other Sports, Family Memories

From the outset CCD was a country club with a golf emphasis. But other sports (as distinct from lesser ones) have left indelible marks on the club's first fifty years.

The importance of bloodlines in determining athletic potential is well understood. Genetic and environmental factors each play a role. At CCD family success patterns seem disproportionately strong.

Kathy Brameier, girls' swimming champion in 1967 and 1968, 1970 through 1974.

If people named Stelben and Zangrillo have been dominant on the golf course, and even as other families can point to remarkable individual achievements at the club, the Brindley clan no doubt deserves to be called "CCD's Best All-Around Athletes." They've demonstrated consistent excellence ever since late patriarch, Aud Brindley, starred for the New York Knicks at Madison Square Garden in the years after World War II.

Aud's widow, Velma (Vel), won the paddle tennis and women's golf crowns in 1965, took the ladies' tennis championship in 1966 and 1967, and almost two decades later won three consecutive ladies' golf titles. She's also a champion bowler. Son David was the boys' swimming champion in 1965 and 1967, and in 1970 teamed with Pat Murphy, Lee Osborn, and Alan Clough to set the boys' 200-yard freestyle relay mark, one that still stands. He was also a noted cross-country runner and low-handicap golfer who won six Al Hetrick Platform Tennis Championships between 1977 and 1988. David was also the 2006 CCD golf champion. David's wife Maggie was

George and Stebby Clough, August 1972.

Alan Clough, 1969.

twice a golf champion at CCD and is the only woman ever to eagle the 3rd Hole. His sister Pamela was junior tennis champion five times in six years in the 1960s.

Jim and Connie Brameier, charter members of CCD, raised four of its best swimmers. From 1961 through 1974 it seemed one or another of the Brameier children (Ann, Mary Lou, Jeff, Kathy) was grabbing an aquatic award. Kathy took the girls' title seven times in eight years. Mary Lou also found time during the swimming season (Memorial Day until early September at CCD) to capture two junior girls' golf championships. The Gerken children (Ann, Meg, Danny) gave the Brameiers a close battle for family honors in those same years. In more recent years Meghan Faughnan and brother Kevin have been dominant.

Alan and Kelly Clough were another brother/sister team to win honors at the pool. They benefited from guidance from mother Stebby, to whom

CCD 2001 Swim Team. Courtesy of the CCD newsletter, September 2001 edition.

Patrick Swift, pool director, at the 1997 CCD Championships.

all swimmers at CCD are in fact deeply indebted. Stebby Clough and her husband George did more than cheer kids on; long after Alan and Kelly had grown up and left the nest, Stebby could be found organizing meets and assisting a succession of swimming coaches at the club.

Since 1991 Pat Swift has been the pool director and head swim coach. He was a summer swimmer as a youth and played lacrosse and tennis in college. Pat was a teacher and dean of students at a middle school in the South Bronx for about ten years, before becoming a school administrator in Port Chester, New York. He coached lacrosse and swimming at New Rochelle High School for the better part of ten years. During the winter he coaches at the nationally recognized "Badger Swim Club" in his spare time. Pat truly embraces his philosophy that summer swimming must be fun. Pat is married to Jacki Swift, the former summer camp director, and has four young children Michael, Kali, Grace, and Matthew.

Karl Levanat now handles tennis and paddle tennis alike as CCD's pro and runs a tennis camp for members' children in the summer. Inter-club matches are important fixtures in the tennis season, both for the younger set and their mothers. The competitive ladder, occasionally the source of controversy, seems to have been supplanted by more informal play among women members. But their tennis team is still active and has been known to cross the border for matches against New Canaan Country Club.

It's reasonable to imagine that the era of single-family dominance of the various sports at CCD could have passed into history. The nuclear family itself has become something of a dinosaur. Latchkey children are often left to make their own decisions, and young people generally have more options than was the case even a generation ago. But thanks to devoted parents and staff, CCD, more than many clubs of comparable size and diversity, has given future generations of members a solid foundation in competitive athletics. This pattern can be observed on Sunday afternoons at the club, where entire families are often seen practicing golf together at the range.

These two young ladies are in the middle of a game.

Young boy working on his putting skills.

OUR MANAGERS
by Tucker Scott, Jr.

PAUL DOYON 1957–1972

Paul was the manager from the outset of the club in 1957. He was a shy, stout, French Canadian and exhibited a seriousness of purpose in exercising his duties. Rules and regulations were made not to be broken.

One day, Tom Butcher was practice putting on the 18th Green at a time the course was idle. CCD was in the throes of constructing a new practice green after the old one had been obliterated to make way for the new curling rink. Tom was aware that practice was permitted only on the practice area, but a practice green was non-existent at the time.

Doyon, observing the infraction of the rules, proceeded in his diplomatic manner and demanded in his French Canadian accent to "get off the green!" Without a response, Tom with his powerful, husky frame grabbed Paul with a firm, forceful grip around his waist and hurled him into the nearby sand trap. Without a word, Doyon climbed out, put his arm around Tom's shoulder and they became fast friends from that day on!

BOB HOLIDAY 1972–1979

A hotel management school graduate, Bob's experience ran the gamut of managing clubs and hotels from Connecticut to Florida. He was a solid operator who sandwiched in subtle wit when he deemed it appropriate but in a low-key straight-faced manner.

For example, after a member's daughter had her wedding reception at the club, the father, concerned about the size of the tab, asked Bob about the bill which had not been received. Bob's reply, "I don't have the final total, Sir. The accounting department is still adding it up."

JIM HUTCHINSON 1979–1989

Jim was symbolic of the typical club manager with experience to expedite all matters pertaining to the operation of a country club. He was weaned from Wee Burn where he was assistant manager, as well as manager of the club.

Jim Hutchinson with Derek Dalrymple, assistant manager.

A good golfer, he flew his own airplane and was a real professional in every respect. This gentleman was well liked by the members. His retirement to Florida paved the way for the next manager.

IAN D. N. FETIGAN 1989–2000

Ian was born in the business. It's in his blood. His family has owned and operated resorts in Bermuda all of his life. To add frosting on the cake, he came to the United States and graduated from the University of Maryland's Hotel and Management School.

Ian D. N. Fetigan.

After that, he joined the staff of the Westchester Country Club and then became assistant manager of Brae Burn Country Club in Purchase, New York. He came to CCD after spending five years as general manager of Pelham Country Club.

Ian's arrival was coincidental with the groundwork for the member-owned club's first five year plan and he coordinated each phase along with his regular duties of managing the club's normal activities.

KEN KOCH 2000–2007

Ken served the hospitality industry for over thirty years. He began his career with the Marriott Corporation in 1976 as kitchen manager and chef. Ken became a general manager with Marriott's Dinner House division in 1982 and opened numerous new facilities throughout Pennsylvania, New Jersey, and Connecticut. Ken served Marriott and then Host International, W. R. Grace and Gilbert Robinson through acquisitions until 1987. Ken opened the Whitman Restaurant in Farmington, Connecticut, in 1987 and served as a general managing partner until 1999. Following his passion for hospitality and sports, in 1999 Ken accepted the position as clubhouse manager of the Country Club of Darien, becoming the general manager in 2000. While at Darien, Ken had oversight of numerous capital projects such as the ballroom and mixed grill, satellite kitchen, and board room. He also was instrumental in the planning stages of the current master plan, which began in 2007. Ken became a certified club manager after successfully

Ken Koch.

completing study at Georgia State University, Cal Poly Pomona, Michigan State University, and the Highland College in Dornoch, Scotland.

After leaving CCD in 2007, Ken accepted the position of general manager at Maidstone Club, a platinum club in East Hampton, New York. Ken is an avid golfer, enjoys travel as well as having a passion for wine and great food.

PAUL KRUZEL 2007–PRESENT

Paul comes to the Country Club of Darien after serving as the acting general manager and director of operations of the Jonathan Club in Los Angeles, California. Paul began his career with Westin Hotels and was the proprietor and chef for the Arlington Inn in Arlington, Vermont. Amongst other positions, Paul has been the vice president for Universal Studios Hollywood CityWalk, Universal Studios Hollywood Theme Park, and Boston Restaurant Associates.

Paul holds a BA in hotel/restaurant and institutional management from Michigan State University and an AOS in culinary arts from Johnson and Wales University in Providence, Rhode Island. He has been the recipient of multiple silver awards from the American Culinary Federation. Paul is a member of the advisory board of the California School of Culinary Arts-Le Cordon Bleu-Pasadena, a member of the National Preservation Historic Trust, and is a past director for "Taste of Vermont" culinary competition.

Paul Kruzel.

CHAPTER
7

Memorable Moments on the Golf Course

Golf history fanatics love to invoke magical moments from the past, even many that happened before they were born. At the Country Club in Brookline, Massachusetts, members still wax sentiment over the astonishing U.S. Open victory of teenaged amateur Francis Ouimet (whose caddy, Eddie Lowery, was ten years old!) over renowned British professionals Harry Vardon and Ted Ray in 1913. Bobby Jones's tying putt on the 18th Green at Winged Foot in 1929, leading to an Open playoff win, sealed his legend even before he went on to win the Grand Slam in 1930. Gene Sarazen brought the Masters Tournament into prominence in 1935 (albeit it wasn't yet called the Masters) with an amazing double eagle on the 15th Hole in the final round. And who hasn't seen the classic photo of Ben Hogan at Merion in 1950, the year after his near-fatal car accident, sending a one-iron approach shot to the 18th Green, leading to a U.S. Open playoff win?

The true genius behind CCD's signature 3rd Hole, golfing great, Gene Sarazen.

Long-time members of CCD maintain their own archive of pleasant memories. These survive not through TV broadcasts or *Golf Digest* articles but through reminiscence.

Golf immortal Gene Sarazen visited the club not long after it's opening. After making an easy birdie on the third hole with a wedge approach and putt, he suggested lengthening it by moving the green to the left and converting the creek that guarded the green into a pond. Sarazen sensed correctly that this would put a greater premium on both the drive and approach shot and toughen Hole 3; today, it's the signature hole at CCD.

Ladies' Professional Golf Association immortal Patty Berg hosted a clinic at CCD in the 1960s. "The King," Arnold Palmer, came to Darien in 1972 and 1973. Palmer's visits are remembered for his having eagled the difficult 16th Hole during an exhibition round, after reaching the green with two mighty shots.

Possibly the most remarkable eighteen holes ever played at CCD was by member Frank McCracken in May 1980. An 11-handicapper, McCracken and three others went out for a friendly round that became something quite special. Frank went around in 5-under par 67 (net 56), establishing an amateur course record that has since been tied but never broken. Memo to weekend golfers: Keep swinging. A miraculous round is always possible.

In order of importance, the highlights of every golf season at CCD are the club championship in August; the Old Tom Morris member/guest, a three-day, forty-five hole tournament held in July; and the member/member tourney in June. Several past club championships are especially well remembered.

Robert (Bobby) Stelben, Jr., grew up as a caddy at CCD. He later learned his craft under Ed Nicholson, whom he credits (along with his dad) with developing his game to championship caliber. After winning six consecutive titles between 2000 and 2005, Bobby and sister Michelle (winner of four consecutive

Old Tom Morris Champions John Mahoney and Bob Herdman. Courtesy of the CCD newsletter, August 2001 edition.

Edgar Auchincloss passes along some wisdom to Arnie.

Brother and sister Bob and Michelle Stelben each won a championship trophy in 2000, the only time this has happened in CCD history. It was Bob's first Men's Championship and Michelle's fourth time as the women's champ. Courtesy of the CCD newsletter, Summer 2000 edition.

women's championships from 1997 to 2000, four earlier girls' titles, and holder of the women's course record with a 72) could reasonably claim for the Stelbens the mantle of "most dominant golf family" at CCD. The Zangrillo clan, holder of four separate titles, would rank a close second.

Bobby had paid his dues before winning his first title, losing two times in the finals. Once he led Dick Ettinger by three holes on the final nine, only to settle for runner-up after Ettinger rallied. When he finally started winning, though, Bobby's knack for holing shots from the fairway made him virtually unbeatable.

In 2004 Stelben was matched against long-hitting Alex Noujaim, who found he was battling more than a dominant opponent. It seems Alex's caddy had divided loyalties. At the 10th Hole during the afternoon round, Bobby's perfectly struck second shot with a sand wedge flew toward the pin. A familiar cry from TV, "Go in the hole," could be heard, and lo and behold that's exactly what the ball did for an eagle two. The match was over. Alex settled for runner-up, and his disappointment was hardly assuaged by the fact

2002 Men's Club Champion Bob Stelben, Jr., with Runner-Up Richard Ettinger. Courtesy of the CCD newsletter, October/November 2002 edition.

that the shout of "Go in!" had come not from the gallery, but from his own caddy! Ah, sportsmanship.

The following year Bobby faced Brian Clark in the finals. Bobby was well ahead beginning the afternoon round but gave Brian momentary hope on the 2nd Hole by turning over the sod on his second shot and moving the ball about ten yards. The fat shot stunned his supporters in the gallery, but Bobby then proceeded to hole out his third from 65 yards and close out the match, thus validating Ed Nicholson's emphasis on the mental side of golf, i.e., "Forget your last shot, no matter how awful it was, and concentrate on the next one." How often do average players give in to exasperation and follow a missed shot with two or three just as bad?

In 1974 Bill San Fan Andre, who had won six consecutive titles between 1966 and 1971, faced off in the thirty-six-hole match-play final against Dick Pressler, then seeking his first club championship. After the morning eighteen holes it looked to everyone as if "Sandie" had met his match. Pressler led 4-up when the contestants broke for lunch.

Former eight-time Men's Club Champion Bill "Sandie" San Fan Andre with now seven-time winner Robert Stelben, Jr. Courtesy of the CCD newsletter, September 2001 edition.

Golf historians in the gallery didn't need a long memory to recall that Arnold Palmer had led Billy Casper by five strokes with just nine holes to play in the U.S. Open at San Francisco's Olympic Club in 1966, only to falter down the stretch and eventually lose to Casper in a playoff. Negative thoughts seem to lurk in a dark corner of every golfer's brain; even the best players can occasionally lose concentration, tense up, and discover their smooth swings have vanished. When this occurs in match play, a savvy opponent will sense it and gain an adrenaline rush.

This clearly happened with Dick Pressler and Bill San Fan Andre, although not immediately. The front nine in the afternoon looked like more of the same.

Birdies at Holes 6 and 7 enabled Pressler to extend his lead to six holes at the turn. Sandie birdied Hole 10, but still trailed by five holes with six to go. Dick needed to win one hole or halve two and a coveted championship was his.

But he bogeyed the long 13th, losing to San Fan Andre's par, went over the green and out of bounds on the 14th for another bogey, then failed to get up and down from a bunker on Hole 15 while San Fan Andre made his par. Sandie wasn't doing anything spectacular, but winning holes with clutch par-saving putts was now proving to be enough. Dick's downward slide continued on Hole 16, when he went over the green with his third and his ten-foot par putt slipped by the cup. Sandie two-putted for a par. He was now one down.

But on Hole 17 it appeared the match was over. Pressler's long iron found the green, twenty feet from the cup, while San Fan Andre was short of the green. In a classic match play-style reversal, Sandie chipped to within six feet and sank his putt, while Dick's three-footer missed…three putts, yet another bogey. Now the match was even, incredibly enough, and on Hole 18 San Fan Andre administered the coup de grace by reaching the green in two with a four-wood from the right rough while Pressler was forced to chip out from the left rough. After his third shot left him still short of the green, Dick conceded the match.

Without making a single birdie on the last six holes, Bill San Fan Andre had somehow managed to overcome a five-hole deficit and win the match in regulation. Arnold Palmer, Greg Norman (in hindsight), and thousands of lesser players could have commiserated with Dick Pressler at that moment.

Dick Ettinger, Sr., holds the all-time record at CCD with eleven club championships and was runner-up another nine times. Dick remembers the San Fan Andre-Pressler match, which he followed from the gallery. He also recalled his own tense finals matches against Wayne Walker, a five-time club champion himself. Ettinger, who still plays to a low single digit handicap, has scored an amazing nine holes-in-one, including an ace on every par-3 hole at CCD (a solitary distinction, needless to say). Dick shot 69 at his winter-home championship course in Jupiter Hills, Florida, not long ago, beating his age with plenty to spare in a round that featured two eagles on par-4 holes. What is it about great players that they hole out from the fairway so often?

1991 Champion Wayne Walker with Runner-Up Dick Ettinger, Sr.

Ettinger stands all of five feet four inches tall. Dick won his first golf title, the junior amateur, at age eighteen in Schenectady, New York, fifty-six years ago. He remembers driving the ball 270 yards with regularity in those days, using an upright swing that seemed to defy the laws of geometry and physics. Ben Hogan, Gary Player, and other great players of short stature swung the club in a flat plane to create the widest possible arc and maximize distance. Can a short man swing the club vertically, a la Jack Nicklaus or Davis Love III, and prosper? Evidently it can be done. Dick isn't as long off the tee these days, but in all modesty he does admit to being "the greatest putter that ever was." Eleven disappointed runners-up from CCD club championship finals over the years could attest to that.

CHAPTER
8

The Members Acquire the Club

From its outset the Country Club of Darien had operated under a lease with Keewaydin Corporation, which owned the land and capital stock of the club. The lease was scheduled to expire in 1999. By 1985 many existing and prospective members had become concerned that only thirteen-plus years remained on the lease. Edgar Auchincloss was in his mid-seventies. What would the future bring?

The decade of the 1980s provided an apt backdrop for the possible acquisition of a club by its membership. Supply-side economics enabled relatively easy capital formation through low interest rates. Vigorous stock and bond markets had enriched the bottom lines of many existing and future members. People "felt richer." And rumors were circulating that Japanese interests actively sought golf properties in Darien. The time was ripe, so in the summer of 1985 Club President Paul Caswell assembled an ad hoc committee to explore an acquisition. He joined a group drawn from the Board of Governors that was chaired by Gay Land and included Ralph Bosch and Phil Coviello.

Phil Coviello, a retired mergers-and-acquisitions lawyer who was president of the member-owned club in 1990–1991, now lives in Santa Fe, New Mexico. He recalled details of the transaction.

"We dealt separately with Keewaydin Corporation for the land itself, and with Edgar Auchincloss personally for the club's assets, such as furniture, china, and silverware," Coviello said. Arriving at an agreed purchase price wasn't simply a matter of assessing a fair value for the property and billing the membership for its pro-rata shares of the total, Phil emphasized. The committee demanded a contingency clause requiring that $3.5 million be raised from members; when added to a mortgage it brought the contingent offer to $7.25 million, which became the agreed

price in the end. The committee was adamant that no fewer than 270 members (90 percent) must subscribe for the sake of unity, and further that the subscription amount per member not exceed the initiation fee of the costliest rival club in town. That happened to be $13,000. "We backed into the numbers," Phil commented. Happily, for each member who declined to participate and resigned voluntarily, someone from the waiting list stood ready to contribute $13,000. Each subscriber received a $10,000 bond and a $3,000 equity certificate.

The "transition" team from family–run to member–owned country club. Past presidents (left to right): Phil Coviello, Tom McGrath, Gay Land, Tom Byrne, Ralph Bosch, Paul Caswell.

The sale price was considerably less than a developer logically would have paid (51 homes could have been built on the 140 acres), but Mrs. Catherine Agnew Auchincloss, Edgar's mother, had always expressed a wish that the one-time Keewaydin Farm remain "open land"... golf course yes, houses no. The family was willing to sell at a sacrifice to be assured of this, and the committee reciprocated with a long-term guarantee in the contract. Other acreage adjoining the club entrance was offered for sale but did not become part of the final agreement.

Paul Caswell was president of the club in 1985 and was involved in the early negotiations with Edgar Auchincloss. From his summer home in Rye Beach, New Hampshire, Paul recalled the complicated process. "I'd been on the Board of Governors for three years before becoming president," Caswell said. "The question of a members' takeover had arisen often at board meetings, but before 1985 it was thought that Edgar wasn't ready to sell or that the membership wasn't ready to buy." But of the fifteen board members, only one or two were opposed in 1985; this called for at least exploring the matter fully. As Paul put it, "We had three choices...do nothing, renew the lease, or have the members buy the club." The first amounted to postponing the inevitable. The second was impractical. So an ad hoc committee was formed to explore the third.

Takeovers and corporate restructurings were an everyday occurrence on Wall Street in the 1980s. But Paul Caswell and others on the board had never been involved in a membership takeover of any country club. Paul wanted all the advice he could get, so he went to the expedient of asking the United States Golf Association in New Jersey for advice. They're more accustomed to handling rules questions or ticket orders for the U.S. Open, but as it happened a nearby club had just been through the same process; Paul was given the name of the right person to call, and he obtained valuable guidance.

Confidentiality was paramount. If word leaked out that a buyout was in the offing, it might invite competition. Near unanimity among the members was needed. A complete proposal package detailing the legal and financial issues was therefore prepared and delivered to all members at once, who then were asked to vote quickly.

"I had no idea how it would be received," Caswell said recently. "I remember arriving at the club the Saturday after the proposals had gone out. About twenty members were waiting outside the locker room for Edgar to open the door (it remained locked until 7:30 a.m. every day back then). One of them said to me, 'Paul, you'd better check your locker for a bomb.' 'Oh, no,' I thought. Fortunately, he was kidding. One by one the members thanked me and said, 'It's about time.' I was relieved."

Edgar Auchincloss had run the club in a patriarchal, hands-on manner for almost thirty years. Under the new circumstances responsibility for decisions would be diffused. A five-year financial plan was put forth, along with a mandate for diversity in membership (another New York-area club whose membership was top-heavy with stockbrokers had folded during an earlier bear market). Now that matters were no longer being left in the hands of one person, proactive communication among disparate interests within the club was vital.

The takeover was approved and implemented. Later in 1986 a black-tie dinner was held at the club to celebrate. For Paul Caswell personally, there followed an ironic twist. In 1987 he was transferred to New Jersey by his employer and had to resign from CCD before witnessing the fruits of his labors. But the club he subsequently joined in New Jersey was later bought out by Japanese interests, at which point Paul realized the rumors he'd heard had been factual and that CCD had done the right thing at the right time.

CHAPTER
9

The Golf Course in 2007...
A Hole-by-Hole Tour

When the present author first toured CCD's eighteen holes in a golf cart in May 2007, he observed an attractive layout of seemingly moderate difficulty…not overly long or punitive, one that professionals would no doubt devour. After playing the course twice in the following week, he saw things quite differently. It's a true test for golfers of every skill level, one that plays longer than the yardages on the card, with small greens that slope in every direction and are well guarded by sand traps, and with gnarly rough that's tougher to play from than it looks. And somehow, the course seemed to play into the wind on every hole.

The accompanying photos reveal some, but hardly all, of the subtleties architect Alfred Horace Tull built into the course. The following text describes the layout from one (average) player's perspective. Distances cited are from the white (middle) tees.

Home pro Mario Laureti set the course record at 64 (eight under par) in 1959. It hasn't been equaled. In regional qualifying events over the years, visiting professionals typically have been happy with scores around par; others have gone home frustrated by CCD's subtleties.

Its eighteen holes are unique in that none begins or ends very far from the clubhouse. This is good news in the event of a sudden cloudburst. The compactness of the layout, however, has presented certain problems.

HOLE	1	2	3	4	5	6	7	8	9	OUT		10	11	12	13	14	15	16	17	18	IN	TOT	HCP	NET
BLUE TEES	360	383	438	370	192	562	194	400	510	3409		361	152	425	602	397	412	520	231	422	3522	6931		
WHITE TEES	348	357	411	359	169	539	184	388	500	3255		352	132	390	555	371	397	508	207	386	3298	6553		
GOLD TEES	342	305	312	338	129	476	126	302	475	2805		322	117	368	508	315	322	486	190	350	2978	5783		
HANDICAP	14	10	2	8	18	4	16	6	12			9	17	5	1	11	7	13	15	3				
PAR	4	4	4	4	3	5	3	4	5	36		4	3	4	5	4	4	5	3	4	36	72		
RED TEES	340	297	300	280	112	472	120	288	410	2619		319	114	363	505									
RED/GOLD HDCP	10	14	6	8	18	2	16	12	4			11	17	5	1									

PLAYER:

USGA SLOPE RATING		USGA COURSE RATING		CHECK TEES PLAYED
Blue Tees	136	Blue Tees	73.5	☐ Blue
White Tees	134	White Tees	71.5	☐ White
Gold Tees	126	Gold Tees	67.8	☐ Gold
Red Tees	128	Red Tees	72.1	☐ Red

DATE:

SCORER:

ATTEST:

CCD scorecard.

Country Club of Darien

Founded, 1957

DARIEN, CT

HOLE 1

Par 4, 348 yards. A straight drive (ideally, slightly from right to left) to the top of a hill sets up a short-iron approach to a well-trapped green sloping from back to front. But like a sword of Damocles, a large tree overhangs the fairway from the left rough in the preferred landing area, coaxing the player to drive to the right for safety. Except that route isn't really safe because the fairway itself banks from left to right toward difficult rough. Even after a "safe" drive that stays in the fairway on the right, the second shot must be played from a sidehill lie with the ball below the golfer's feet. Not a backbreaking hole to start a round, but not an easy one, either.

HOLE 2

Par 4, 357 yards. This is an unusual hole. The tee is elevated, but the ground slopes upward from it, so the tee shot is partially blind. From a fairly wide landing area the fairway and rough slope from right to left; a long, straight drive will reach the bottom (Steve Zangrillo once drove the green), setting up a short-iron approach. It isn't a long hole, but the green has subtle breaks that make birdies elusive.

HOLE 3

Par 4, 393 yards. This is the signature hole at CCD, one whose present design resulted from a recommendation by the legendary Gene Sarazen. A dogleg left with a large fairway bunker at the right corner, it calls for a right-to-left drive of sufficient length to reach the bottom of a hill shaping the bend in the fairway. A short drive, or one to the right rough or in the trap at the corner, mandates a lay-up approach because the green is fully guarded by a pond. Even after a good drive and a second shot over the pond, the player has work to do. The two-level green slopes severely from back to front; a putt from behind the hole can easily roll to the front, while a long uphill putt from the front to a back pin position must reach the second tier. Par is a great score here.

HOLE 4

Par 4, 366 yards. Uphill all the way, Hole 4 plays longer than the yardage on the card. The driving area is wide, but left-center of the fairway is best for a clear shot with a mid-iron to a smallish green. From the right side of the fairway or right rough, the green sits behind a yawning trap. Taking enough club for the approach is vital here, and once reaching the green the golfer has to deal with subtle breaks on the putting surface.

HOLE
5

Par 3, 148 yards. Downhill to a wide but fairly shallow green protected by two bunkers on the left/front and a lake behind, this par-3 calls for a lofted short-iron shot. A trapped iron forces an explosion shot toward the water, which is visually intimidating. The hole looks easy from the cart path, but plays harder from the tee despite its relative shortness. The green slopes sharply from left to right. Par is a good score.

HOLE 6

Par 5, 549 yards. A dogleg right par-5 with a tee shot over water, Hole 6 is a classic risk-reward hole. Since even long hitters can't reach the green in two, there's more risk than reward in shortening the hole by aiming right, but a "too safe" drive can go through the fairway into rough on the left. Once in the fairway off the tee, the hole is fairly straightforward, with an ample landing area for the blind second shot over a gentle hill. The third shot is played downhill to a fairly deep but narrow green that tilts from back to front and isn't easy to putt.

HOLE 7

Par 3, 152 yards. An innocuous short hole, its key challenge is club selection from the tee. Slightly downhill, Hole 7 is one of the few holes at CCD that plays shorter than its stated yardage. Tall trees surround the green, which protect iron shots from the wind but also make judging distance difficult.

HOLE 8

Par 4, 393 yards. An outstanding par-4 hole, Hole 8 is a 90-degree dogleg to the right. A large trap at the neck of the dogleg calls for a 230-yard carry to reach the narrow fairway beyond, leaving a downhill mid-iron approach that plays longer than the golfer thinks. A drive to the left of the fairway bunker leaves a long second shot, a drive too far right lands among trees and usually forces a lay-up shot back to the fairway.

HOLE
9

Par 5, 500 yards. Another dogleg right, risk-reward par-5 hole that invites alternate strategies depending on the golfer's skill and daring. A powerful drive with a slight fade can encourage a long hitter to go for the green in two, but the second shot over a creek can't stray left or right because the green is so small that any third shot from an angle, even with a sand wedge, won't hold it. An average hitter has to guard against going left off the tee because three fairway traps can swallow a drive and make clearing the creek on the second shot a problem. A weak drive might not reach the fairway.

HOLE 10

Par 4, 352 yards. A pretty hole and a slight dogleg to the right that plays harder than it looks. The tee shot should favor the left side toward trees and rough. This opens up the approach, and even drives that land in the rough will often bounce rightward into the fairway. However, this can leave a sidehill lie. A drive too far right will leave a blocked second shot. The small green is well trapped and not easy to putt.

HOLE
11

Par 3, 132 yards. A short, uphill par-3 framed by a manor house and tall trees, Hole 11 is picturesque. It looks fairly easy from the tee, but the green is guarded by deep traps on the left and right, so its narrowness makes sand saves difficult regardless of the pin position. The long green also slopes from front to back, a subtlety that isn't visible from the tee. Local knowledge helps here, and three-putt greens are common.

HOLE
12

Par 4, 390 yards. A slight dogleg left from an elevated tee, Hole 12 is an excellent driving hole. It plays shorter than the yardage on the card, but the drive must avoid trees and rough on the left and a pond on the right. Once in the fairway, which narrows at the dogleg, the player is faced with an iron approach, slightly uphill to a large and deep green, open in the front. The green slopes from back to front; putts from below the hole must be struck firmly.

HOLE 13

Par 5, 555 yards. A true three-shot par-5, Hole 13 will test a golfer's long game, especially into the prevailing wind. There's ample room off the tee, but a short drive or one finding the rough presents real problems because the second shot must clear an angled creek to reach the fairway beyond, after which the hole bends to the left and slopes gently downhill to a smallish green, trapped on both sides. The tricky green has a back-right-to-front-left slope, and seems closer from the fairway than it really is, making club selection for the third shot pivotal. Unlike many par-5s, this isn't a birdie hole.

HOLE
14

Par 4, 371 yards. This is a very deceiving par-4. Straightaway with plenty of room off the tee, it looks like a birdie opportunity at first glance. But the green is very shallow and firm, so the approach with a short- or mid-iron must be well lofted; there's out-of-bounds beyond the green and traps in front. Especially downwind, a second shot without enough backspin can easily go over the green, leading to a downhill pitch from difficult rough at best, a stroke-and-distance penalty at worst.

HOLE
15

Par 4, 397 yards. Another hole that plays longer than the scorecard yardage, Hole 15 calls for a well struck drive uphill to a rolling fairway with traps and out-of-bounds on the left and rough and trees on the right. The best tee shot favors the left side of the fairway, setting up a medium-to-long-iron approach, slightly downhill, to a green protected by a large and deep bunker on the right front. The green is well sloped with a false front; it demands a second shot that carries all the way to the putting surface.

HOLE
16

Par 5, 508 yards. Once eagled by Arnold Palmer, Hole 16 is an unusual par-5, a double-dogleg to the right with fairway traps on the left, a wide creek to clear on the second shot, and another large trap strategically guarding the second fairway on the left. Because the tiny green must be approached from the left, that bunker comes into play. Unlike many par-5 holes, length off the tee isn't essential. But played conservatively, it's still a challenge because of a small, well-trapped green that calls for a precise third shot.

HOLE
17

Par 3, 207 yards. Slightly downhill to a large green open in the front, Hole 17 isn't a tricky hole, but its raw length calls for a wood or long iron from the tee, after which the player has to negotiate subtle breaks on the green. Par is a good score on Hole 17.

HOLE 18

Par 4, 386 yards. Beautifully designed and challenging, the finishing hole at CCD gives even a low-handicap player a lot to handle. Into the wind, it's a brute. Any drive to the left side, no matter how long, sets up a difficult approach to an elevated green guarded by a large tree overhanging the fairway from the rough. A drive to the right must carry 225 yards to clear a strategically placed fairway bunker; that's the open route home, but the approach must still clear a yawning trap that appears to guard the green but is actually well short of it. This tempts the player to underclub on the second shot. The large and severely sloped green makes the approach putt crucial here. It's a par-4 on the scorecard, but one careless shot on Hole 18 can lead to a double-bogey or worse.

CHAPTER
10

Preparing the Club for the Next Fifty Years

Golf courses evolve. Even Augusta National and Pinehurst have been redesigned or tweaked over the years to make them more challenging, less vulnerable to weather variables, and better for spectator viewing and/or TV coverage. CCD's Board wrestled with the twin concerns of challenge and weather vulnerability for an extended period of time. The decision was made in 2005 to engage Golf Course Architect Mike Hurdzan to develop a plan to renovate the golf course. Alterations commenced in 2007 and are scheduled for completion in 2009, which will incorporate other modifications to the facility that have been considered for years. Head Professional Ed Nicholson, who manages golf activity at CCD with aplomb and with invaluable help from long-time assistant Neil Lovelady and veteran caddy master Nick Holowiak, kindly briefed the author on plans for the next two years.

Hawkshaw's Andy Stevens and Mr. Bob Herdman. Courtesy of the CCD Newsletter, August 2008 edition.

Hole 10 is a pretty par-4, a slight dogleg right that tracks northward from a tee next to the clubhouse entrance road to an elevated green 352 yards away. But many golfers slice their tee shots; the parking lot to the right of Hole 10 has seen its share of out-of-bounds drives over the years, with all that implies for the risk to members and their guests, to parked cars, even for bemused insurance adjusters from Blue Cross and GEICO.

What to do? Direct the hole more to the left, toward the current second tee, thus creating a sharper dogleg. The green will stay put, making the hole a tad harder perhaps, but the important advantage is that it will take the parking lot out of play once and for all.

Change begets change. Moving the fairway on Hole 10 will require a makeover of what is now Hole 2, a southbound par-4 that adjoins Hole 10 because long drives off the new Hole 10, especially if pulled or hooked, would imperil golfers walking off the second tee. So the present Hole 2's tee will be moved forward, creating an exciting downhill par-3 hole with distances ranging from 165 to 215 yards.

Sliced drives have also created a hazardous situation for players on the 18th fairway. There's no hole to the right of Hole 18, but there's a practice area, and for years players lining up approach shots to Hole 18 green from the right side of the fairway have had to dodge wayward

Hole 7 (old 16th).

shots from the range. Occasionally the reverse happens, and a lesson is interrupted by a cry of "Fore" and the flight of an errant Titleist from Hole 18.

So the green on Hole 18 will be moved thirty to forty yards to the left, and the practice area will be redesigned into a semi-circular shape and enlarged, even as the landing area is narrowed. The new conical-shaped range should further please insurance carriers.

Hole 16 is now a double-dogleg right. Arnold Palmer once eagled it with a long drive to the extreme left of the fairway, taking advantage of a (then) clear path to the green from that side. But trees have grown up since 1972 that now impede Palmer's chosen route home; the hole is now a three-shot par-5 whose shape frustrates low-handicap players who have to lay up twice and thus forfeit their advantage of the length off the tee.

So Hole 16 will become a par-4 with a single dogleg to the right. The green, which will be moved up to hug the creek on the right, will also

Hole 18 (old 9th).

Hole 7 (old 16th).

have to be remodeled. It's tiny, and in its present shape wouldn't hold even a well struck second shot from two hundred yards away.

Moving the green on Hole 16 will provide room to lengthen Hole 17, now a long par-3 that some members can't reach from the tee. It will become a risk-reward par-4, only 320 yards or so in length but tricky; this will preserve the respite between longer Holes 16 and 18 while at once allowing shorter hitters to reach Hole 17 green in regulation. With the present Hole 2 now becoming a longish par-3, a welcome variety among CCD's short holes is retained.

Hole 4 (old 13th).

Hole 8 (old 17th).

Except for Holes 1 and 10, the nines are being reversed. Hole 11 will become the new Hole 2, Hole 12 will become Hole 3, and so forth. Similarly, the newly shortened Hole 2 will become Hole 11; the "Sarazen hole" will be Hole 12, etc. Other contemplated changes include: leveling off the present Hole 6 green to allow for a greater variety of pin positions; adding twenty yards to what is now Hole 7 and moving the green further left to create a more challenging par-3 hole; and leveling off the current Hole 8 fairway, which now slopes to the left in the driving area even as the hole doglegs right.

Hole 11 (old 2nd).

Even as the golf course alterations are being made, other renovation projects mandated by a 2006 Master Plan will be underway. As described in a section of the plan headed,

Courtesy of Playbooks for Golf.

New main kitchen.

"Building on the Past," the board cited its desired renovations as being an extension of the process that began with the member's acquisition of the club in 1986. These are keeping with what the board described as "(a) unified, agrarian look that recalls the history of this property and works well within the natural landscape."

A new kitchen will replace the current one. The equipment has aged, and a need exists for a more efficient work environment for the staff. Conformity to current health and safety codes is a must.

The golf course maintenance facility will be replaced or upgraded, as necessitated by safety and environmental considerations. More space is needed to service and store the machinery and equipment used to keep the course shipshape.

The swimming pool has developed structural problems related to age. Since 1991 there has been a steady increase in usage by the members; this has shortened the time horizon for making needed renovations. The upper level of the snack bar will be modernized.

The staff house will be replaced. CCD's history of taking care of its employees well and earning their loyalty can best be preserved by a new facility that meets the club's standards

Even as Hole 10 is being redirected to protect cars in the main parking lot, the lot itself and the driveway leading to it will be modified and repaved. This will be a boon to safety and drainage and will provide added room for the ever-larger vehicles parked there.

New staff house.

APPENDIX
Chairmen of the Board

James J. Cochran
1957–1959

J. Wilson Shaver
1960–1962

Frederick H. Rudolph
1963

Gerald Prentice *
1964–1965, 1969

Clifford W. Isaacson
1966

C. Voss Hutton
1967

James A. Wold
1968

Harry P. Vaughn, Jr.
1970–1972

D. Bruce Wiesley
1973–1975

Samuel W. Tinsley
1976–1977

Lee P. Hindenach
1978–1981

Kenneth D. Rutter
1982–1985

* Gerald Prentice completed Jim Wold's term when Jim was transferred to Chicago.

Paul H. Caswell
1986–1987
(Chairman/President)

Gay V. Land
1987–1988

Ralph A. Bosch
1989

Philip C. Coviello
1990–1991

Thomas E. McGrath
1992–1993

Thomas E. Byrne
1994–1995

Alphonse M. Palmer
1996–1997

John Romanos
1998–1999

Joseph A. Romano
2000–2001

Anthony C. Zangrillo
2002–2003

John H. McClutchy, Jr.
2004

Thomas E. McGrath
2005–2007

Men's Golf Champions

Stephen F. Zangrillo	1957	William San Fan Andre	1974	Wayne C. Walker	1991
John DeGarmo	1958	William F. Whaley	1975	Richard W. Ettinger	1992
James P. Smith	1959	Richard W. Ettinger	1976	Wayne C. Walker	1993
James P. Smith	1960	Richard W. Ettinger	1977	Wayne C. Walker	1994
James P. Smith	1961	William F. Whaley	1978	Wayne C. Walker	1995
Stephen F. Zangrillo	1962	Thomas P. White	1979	Wayne C. Walker	1996
William San Fan Andre	1963	William F. Whaley	1980	Richard W. Ettinger	1997
Dilworth H. Walker	1964	Richard W. Ettinger	1981	Anthony Zangrillo	1998
Gregg Powers	1965	William F. Whaley	1982	Steven Wright	1999
William San Fan Andre	1966	Richard W. Ettinger	1983	Robert Stelben, Jr.	2000
William San Fan Andre	1967	Paul G. Kimball	1984	Robert Stelben, Jr.	2001
William San Fan Andre	1968	Richard W. Ettinger	1985	Robert Stelben, Jr.	2002
William San Fan Andre	1969	Richard W. Ettinger	1986	Robert Stelben, Jr.	2003
William San Fan Andre	1970	Richard W. Ettinger	1987	Robert Stelben, Jr.	2004
William San Fan Andre	1971	Richard W. Ettinger	1988	Robert Stelben, Jr.	2005
J. Brewster Johnson	1972	Daniel P. Mageras	1989	David Brindley	2006
John R. Callow	1973	Richard W. Ettinger	1990	Robert Stelben, Jr.	2007

Left to right: Stephanie Hahn, Women's Club Champion, Robert Stelben, Jr., Men's Club Champion with Runners-Up Brian Clark and Molly Ferm. Courtesy of the CCD newsletter, September 2001 edition.

Dan Mageras, champion, with Paul Kimble, runner-up in 1989.

Women's Golf Champions

Mrs. Allan D. Graves 1958	Mrs. Gary A. Everson 1975	Mrs. Jackie Prentice Leach 1992
Mrs. William D. Lanier 1959	Mrs. Ellis M. Weld, Jr. 1976	Margaret Brindley 1993
Mrs. Allan D. Graves 1960	Mrs. Ellis M. Weld, Jr. 1977	Katherine Roach....................... 1994
Mrs. Allan D. Graves 1961	Mrs. William C. Gow 1978	Sue Epstein.............................. 1995
Mrs. William D. Lanier 1962	Mrs. Jack P. Nelson 1979	Mary Romanos......................... 1996
Mrs. Forbes K. Wilson 1963	Mrs. Ellis M. Weld, Jr. 1980	Michelle Stelben 1997
Mrs. Gerald E. Prentice........... 1964	Mrs. Gary A. Everson 1981	Michelle Stelben 1998
Mrs. Vel Brindley..................... 1965	Mrs. Gary A. Everson 1982	Michelle Stelben 1999
Mrs. Fred Richards.................. 1966	Mrs. Vel Brindley..................... 1983	Michelle Stelben 2000
Mrs. Fred Richards.................. 1967	Mrs. Vel Brindley..................... 1984	Stephanie Hahn 2001
Mrs. Forbes K. Wilson 1968	Mrs. Vel Brindley..................... 1985	Mary Romanos......................... 2002
Mrs. Gerald E. Prentice........... 1969	Mrs. Jerome S. Miller 1986	Mary Romanos......................... 2003
Mrs. Fred Richards.................. 1970	Mrs. Alfred W. Vitale 1987	Stephanie Hahn 2004
Mrs. Richard A. Madden.......... 1971	Mrs. David Brindley 1988	Maggie Brindley 2005
Mrs. David F. Hart 1972	Mrs. Alfred W. Vitale 1989	Sue Epstein.............................. 2006
Mrs. Gary A. Everson 1973	Mrs. Rita Romano................... 1990	Rhea Bischoff........................... 2007
Mrs. Gustavus J. Esselen III 1974	Mrs. Rita Romano................... 1991	

2002 Women's Club Champion Mary Romanos (right) with Runner-Up Maggie Brindley. Courtesy of the CCD newsletter, October/November 2002 edition.

This 1989 photo shows (left to right) Jannet Mageras (1988 runner-up) with Champion Mary Vitale. Back row, left to right: Dan Mageras and Al Vitale.

Senior Men's Golf Champions

Tucker Scott 1993
Bruce Beagley 1994
Dr. Malcolm Graham, Seniors Division 1995
Ric Patrone, Super Seniors
Winsor Watson
Gay Land 1996
John Barna, Seniors Division

Stroke Play		Stableford Points
Phil Coviello	1997	Victor Nochese
Richard Ettinger, Sr.	1998	Russ Peppet
Jim Hahn	1999	Larry Hutchins
Vic Ferrante	2000	George Bello
Neil Falco	2001	Tom Lom
Richard Ettinger, Sr.	2002	Stuart Atha
Robb Peglar	2003	John Barna
Richard Ettinger, Sr.	2004	Ed Shergalis
Nick Friese	2005	John Barna
Brian Clark	2006	Tom Lom
Charles Deluca	2007	John Barna

Ralph and Edie Bosch with the Junior Inter-Club.

1969 Junior Boys' Champion John Geddes, Jr., and David Brindley, runner-up.

Junior Boys and Junior Girls Golf Champions

Girls

Jerro Idine Cole	1960	Michele Perry	1972	No Competition	1984
Kate Batten	1961	Janet Prentico	1973	Michelle Ferrante	1985
Kate Batten	1962	No Competition	1974	Annie Holland	1986
Deborah Haskell	1963	Gina Zangrillo	1975	Michelle Ferrante	1987
Kate Batten	1964	Linda Born Huetter	1976	Michelle Ferrante	1988
Mary Lou Brameier	1965	Jane Madden	1977	Meredith Sicilano	1989
Debbie Haskell	1966	Jane Madden	1978	Michelle Stelben	1990
Mary Lou Brameier	1967	No Competition	1979	Michelle Stelben	1991
Martha Scott	1968	Mary Whaley	1980	Michelle Stelben	1992
Martha Scott	1969	Christine Watson	1981	Michelle Stelben	1993
Sue Madden	1970	Candy Craig	1982		
Sue Madden	1971	No Competition	1983		

Boys

Sherwin Haskell III	1960	Anthony Zangrillo	1973	Phil Caswell	1985
Sherwin Haskell III	1961	Allen Kinkley	1974	Scott Magrath	1986
Sherwin Haskell III	1962	Anthony Zangrillo	1975	Blake Alcock	1987
Peter H. Sternberg	1963	Christopher Madden	1976	Marc Romano	1988
John H. Weyeneth	1964	Anthony Zangrillo	1977	Marc Romano	1989
Gary Powers	1965	Gary Webb	1978	Sloan Saverine	1990
Donald Besken	1966	Tom Whalen	1979	Sloan Saverine	1991
Scott Becken	1967	Brad Silcox	1980	Sloan Saverine	1992
Winsor H. Watson	1968	Brad Silcox	1981	Rob Carr	1993
John A. Geddes, Jr.	1969	Brad Silcox	1982	Rob Carr	1994
John A. Geddes, Jr.	1970	Jeff Heuer	1983	Rob Carr	1995
Wm. San Fan Andre, Jr.	1971	Todd Alcock	1984	Rob Carr	1996
Michael Pyegsler	1972				

Darien Cup

Wee Burn Country Club.......... 1961	Woodway Country Club.......... 1977	Wee Burn Country Club.......... 1992
Woodway Country Club.......... 1962	Woodway Country Club.......... 1978	Country Club of Darien 1993
Woodway Country Club.......... 1963	Wee Burn Country Club.......... 1979	Woodway Country Club.......... 1994
Wee Burn Country Club.......... 1964	Woodway Country Club.......... 1980	Country Club of Darien 1995
Wee Burn Country Club.......... 1965	Country Club of Darien 1981	Country Club of Darien 1996
Country Club of Darien 1966	Woodway Country Club.......... 1982	Woodway Country Club.......... 1997
Wee Burn Country Club.......... 1967	Wee Burn Country Club.......... 1983	Woodway Country Club.......... 1998
Wee Burn Country Club.......... 1968	Woodway Country Club.......... 1984	Woodway Country Club.......... 1999
Wee Burn Country Club.......... 1969	Woodway Country Club.......... 1985	Woodway Country Club.......... 2000
Wee Burn Country Club.......... 1970	Woodway Country Club.......... 1986	Woodway Country Club.......... 2001
Woodway Country Club.......... 1971	Woodway Country Club.......... 1987	Woodway Country Club.......... 2002
Woodway Country Club.......... 1972	Woodway Country Club.......... 1988	Woodway Country Club.......... 2003
Wee Burn Country Club.......... 1973	Woodway Country Club.......... 1989	Country Club of Darien 2004
Woodway Country Club.......... 1974	Country Club of Darien /	Woodway Country Club.......... 2005
No Tournament 1975	Woodway Country Club.......... 1990	Woodway Country Club.......... 2006
Country Club of Darien 1976	Woodway Country Club.......... 1991	Woodway Country Club.......... 2007

San Jan Andre Cup

Richard Pressler—Thomas White............................ 1974	John Howell—Peter Santella, Jr. 1991
Richard Ettinger, Sr.—James Malloy 1975	Lou Annunziato—V. B. Lougee.............................. 1992
Herbert Noren—Thomas Shreve 1976	Robert Stelben, Sr.—Richard Harter 1993
Emerson Carlson—Gus Esselen 1977	Andy Bieler—Tom Juterbock 1994
Joseph Calve—Leslie Gould.................................... 1978	John Ryan—Gary Holloway 1995
Edward O'Rourke—Barry Yager............................. 1979	Tom Albani—Tom McGrath.................................... 1996
Robert Bryson—Sam Tinsley 1980	Tom Albani—Tom McGrath.................................... 1997
Charles Minckler—Ted Slowik 1981	Nick Friese—Don Lay.. 1998
Richard Ettinger, Sr.—John Gaughan...................... 1982	Lou Annunziato—Richard Davies........................... 1999
Richard T. Davies—James C. Hance 1983	Al Ceresa—Jack Fischer.. 2000
Frank Anselmo—Robert J. Flynn 1984	Jack Collins—Ron Srader...................................... 2001
Herbert Noren—Norman F. Ottley 1985	Bob Stelben, Jr.—Craig Powell 2002
Adolph Di Basio—Richard Berry............................ 1986	Stuart Atha III—John King, Jr. 2003
Edward O'Rourke—William Wunder....................... 1987	Steve True—Dennis Zinkand.................................. 2004
Richard Ettinger, Sr.—Ted Slowik.......................... 1988	Pete Wright—Steve Wright.................................... 2005
Philip Coviello—Richard Pressler........................... 1989	John Howell—John King, Jr. 2006
Brian Clark—Michael McLaughlin 1990	Pete Imbrogno—Mike Imbrogno............................. 2007

Men's Tennis Champions

Alvah W. Sulloway 1958	Heinz Riehl 1975	Bill Nutting 1992
Douglas Jay Coyle 1959	Brendan O'Rourke 1976	Chris Gorman.......................... 1993
Douglas Jay Coyle 1960	Samuel W. Tinsley 1977	Chris Gorman.......................... 1994
Douglas Jay Coyle 1961	Heinz Riehl 1978	Bill Nutting 1995
Douglas Jay Coyle 1962	Kevin Frank 1979	Bill Nutting 1996
Douglas Jay Coyle 1963	Brendan O'Rourke 1980	Kent Epply 1997
Robert P. Kraus 1964	Lee Hamilton 1981	Kent Epply 1998
Robert P. Kraus 1965	Lee Hamilton 1982	Kent Epply 1999
Robert P. Kraus 1966	Al Binks 1983	Neil Duncan 2000
Samuel W. Tinsley 1967	Lee Hamilton 1984	Neil Duncan 2001
Samuel W. Tinsley 1968	Lee Hamilton 1985	Scott Watson 2002
Charles D. Parker 1969	Michael Powell 1986	Neil Duncan 2003
Samuel W. Tinsley 1970	Michael Powell 1987	Mike Matheis 2004
Chris Hawes........................... 1971	Michael Powell 1988	John Corcoran 2005
Chris Hawes........................... 1972	Michael Powell 1989	Mike Matheis 2006
No Competition....................... 1973	Todd Hargrove 1990	Chris Gorman.......................... 2007
Heinz Riehl 1974	Larry Gaggero........................ 1991	

Women's Tennis Champions

Mrs. A. C. Caswell 1958	Barbara McLaughlin 1975	Lyn Nevins 1992
Mrs. G. D. Johnston 1959	Kit Reilly................................. 1976	Janis Rehlaender 1993
Mrs. G. D. Johnston 1960	Kit Reilly................................. 1977	Lyn Nevins 1994
Mrs. Walter N. Plaut 1961	Kit Reilly................................. 1978	Janis Rehlaender 1995
Mrs. Walter N. Plaut 1962	Barbara McLaughlin 1979	Janis Rehlaender 1996
Kay Sellery............................. 1963	Marion Weatherstone 1980	Lyn Nevins 1997
Kay Sellery............................. 1964	Nina Dillon............................. 1981	Lyn Nevins 1998
Kay Sellery............................. 1965	Marion Weatherstone 1982	Deidre McAllister 1999
Mrs. Vel Brindley.................... 1966	Marion Weatherstone 1983	Deidre McAllister 2000
Mrs. Vel Brindley.................... 1967	Yvonne Marchal 1984	Lyn Nevins 2001
Mrs. Stephen Zangrillo 1968	Marion Weatherstone 1985	Lyn Nevins 2002
Patricia Mays 1969	Lyn Nevins 1986	Kelly McCoy Newton 2003
Pamela Brindley...................... 1970	Lyn Nevins 1987	Lyn Nevins 2004
Patricia Mays 1971	Lyn Nevins 1988	Kelly McCoy Newton 2005
Mrs. Stephen Zangrillo 1972	Janis Rehlaender 1989	Kelly McCoy Newton 2006
Barbara McLaughlin 1973	Lyn Nevins 1990	Kelly McCoy Newton 2007
Barbara McLaughlin 1974	Marion Weatherstone 1991	

Club championship participants, left to right: Pam Wisinski, Gloria Mullen, Carol Santosus, and Sheryl Lincoln. Courtesy of the CCD newsletter, August 2001 edition.

Junior Boys and Junior Girls Tennis Champions

Boys

Dave Crane	1960	Douglas Cowherd	1973	Brent Gibbons	1986
William Mason	1961	Brenden O'Rourke	1974	Brent Gibbons	1987
Robert P. Kraus	1962	Peter Santella, Jr.	1975	Brent Gibbons	1988
Michael J. Kraus	1963	Peter Santella, Jr.	1976	Brent Gibbons	1989
Richard Geise	1964	Tom Whaley	1977	Patrick Pendergast	1990
John Geddes, Jr.	1965	Tom Whaley	1978	Kyle Raver	1991
Richard Geise	1966	Tom Whaley	1979	Andrew Ayers	1992
John Geddes, Jr.	1967	Tom Whaley	1980	Kyle Raver	1993
Stuart S. Clough	1968	Spencer Grimes	1981	Sam Epstein	1994
John Geddes, Jr.	1969	Alastair Binks	1982	David Clark	1995
John Cleary	1970	Todd Hargrove	1983	Sam Epstein	1996
Lee Arnold	1971	Todd Hargrove	1984		
Douglas Cowherd	1972	Brent Gibbons	1985		

Girls

Kay Sellery	1960				
Kay Sellery	1961				
Sue Casselman	1962				
Mary Brobston	1963				
Pamela Brindley	1964				
Pamela Brindley	1965				
Pamela Brindley	1966				
Pamela Brindley	1967				
Virginia G. Horan	1968				
Pamela Brindley	1969				
Patricia Mays	1970				
Katherine Reilly	1971				
Katherine Reilly	1972				
Julie Hendrickson	1973	Nina Dillon	1978	Christy Mayo	1989
Cheri Abernathy	1974	Nina Dillon	1979	Lauren Busskohl	1990
Cheri Abernathy	1975	Nina Dillon	1980	Lauren Busskohl	1991
Linda Bornhuetter	1976	Christine Lohr	1981	Lauren Busskohl	1992
Cathy Santosus	1977	Heather Binks	1982	Lauren Busskohl	1993
		Mary Whaley	1983	Sarah Matsuzaka	1994
		Kelly Hetrick	1984	Sarah Matsuzaka	1995
		Liz Mason	1985	Chrissy Nevins-Herbert	1996
		Sara Chambers	1986		
		No Competition	1987		
		Wyn Srader	1988		

Parent-child participants: Brian and Donal Hennessy, Brian and Leigh Kosnick with Head Professional Steve Hardin. Courtesy of the CCD newsletter, September 2001 edition.

Al Hetrick Memorial Platform Tennis
Men's and Women's Champions

Men

T. Hariton	A. Hetrick	D. Brindley
J. Geddes 1965	P. Labe 1976	A. Hetrick...............1987
E. Geise	D. Brindley	D. Brindley
W. Smith...............1966	J. Geddes 1977	A. Hetrick...............1988
T. Hariton	J. Geddes	B. Lohr
J. Geddes 1967	P. Labe 1978	S. Wright 1989
T. Hariton	A. Hetrick	S. Wright
J. Geddes 1968	C. Pollard 1979	B. Lohr, Jr...............1990
T. Hariton	A. Hetrick	S. Wright
J. Geddes 1969	C. Pollard 1980	S. Bardwell...............1991
M. Frank	A. Hetrick	A. Bieler
S. Tinsley...............1970	C. Pollard 1981	S. Wright 1992
T. Hariton	A. Hetrick	G. Wyper
J. Geddes 1971	C. Pollard 1982	A. Massie 1993
M. Frank	P. Labe	S. Wright
M. Tinsley 1972	L. Hamilton 1983	A. Bieler 1994
J. Geddes	A. Hetrick	A. Bieler
P. Petrus 1973	C. Pollard 1984	S. Wright 1995
P. Labe	D. Brindley	S. Wright
C. Pietsch 1974	A. Hetrick...............1985	A. Bieler 1996
M. Frank	D. Brindley	
S. Tinsley...............1975	A. Hetrick...............1986	

Women

B. Brown	V. Brindley	M. Labe
D. Holmes 1960	G. Prentice...............1970	Y. Zangrillo 1981
D. Holmes	V. Brindley	M. Labe
S. Plaut 1961	G. Prentice...............1971	Y. Zangrillo 1982
B. Brown	D. Calo	I. Bray
D. Boyle 1962	M. Labe 1972	V. Cooper 1983
D. Holmes	D. Calo	I. Bray
S. Plaut 1963	M. Labe 1973	V. Cooper 1984
V. Brindley	V. Brindley	M. Christman
G. Prentice...............1964	G. Prentice...............1974	V. Murphy 1985
V. Brindley	M. Labe	V. Murphy
G. Prentice...............1965	Y. Zangrillo 1975	B. McLaughlin 1986
V. Brindley	A. Dunlap	V. Cooper
G. Prentice...............1966	N. Steele 1977	V. Murphy 1987
V. Brindley	M. Labe	V. Brindley
G. Prentice...............1967	Y. Zangrillo 1978	V. Cooper 1988
V. Brindley	I. Bray	B. Magrath
G. Prentice...............1968	V. Cooper 1979	J. Morris 1989
D. Holmes	M. Labe	
Y. Zangrillo 1969	Y. Zangrillo 1980	

Boys and Girls Swimming Champions

Boys

Judson Reis	1957
David Stoeckle	1958
Bruce Kraig	1959
Barry Calder	1960
David Stoeckle	1961
David Stoeckle	1962
Daniel E. Hendricks	1963
Jeffrey W. Brameier	1964
David Brindley	1965
Jeffrey W. Brameier	1966
David Brindley	1967
Patrick Murphy	1968
Daniel Gerken	1969
Patrick Murphy	1970
Jeff Castle	1971
Patrick Murphy	1972
Alan Clough	1973
Steve Blount	1974
Kern Fredericks	1975
Chris Biggs	1976
Chris Biggs	1977
Geoff Mullen	1978
Chris Biggs	1979
Andy Mellett	1980
Andy Mellett	1981
Andy Mellett	1982
John Stanley	1983
Greg Bower	1984
John Stanley	1985
John Stanley	1986
John Stanley	1987
David Nava	1988
Paul Stanley	1989
David Nava	1990
David Clark	1991
David Clark	1992
Sam Epstein	1993
Kevin Faughnan	1994
Kevin Faughnan	1995
Kevin Faughnan	1996
Kevin Faughnan	1997
Kevin Faughnan	1998
Kevin Nugent	1999
Kevin Nugent	2000
Kevin Nugent	2001
Chris Calby	2002
Chris Calby	2003
Chris Calby	2004
Chris Calby	2005
Henry Hobbs	2006
Justin Coley	2007

Girls

Ann Brameier	1957
Leslie Baltz	1958
Christine Wold	1959
Janet Meyer	1960
Janet Meyer	1961
Janet Meyer	1962
Jean Collins	1963
Martha Scott	1964
Martha Scott	1965
Martha Scott	1966
Kathy Brameier	1967
Kathy Brameier	1968
Margaret Gerken	1969
Kathy Brameier	1970
Kathy Brameier	1971
Kathy Brameier	1972
Kathy Brameier	1973
Kathy Brameier	1974
Kelley Clough	1975
Kelley Clough	1976
Christine Watson	1977
Debbie Dubrowski	1978
Christine Watson	1979
Kristin Stanley	1980
Christine Watson	1981
Jill McLaughlin	1982
Jill McLaughlin	1983
Jill McLaughlin	1984
Melissa Komlyn	1985
Kim Henry	1986
Melissa Komlyn	1987
Penny O'Kelley	1988
No Champion	1989
Penny O'Kelley	1990
Leslie Graham	1991
Meghan Faughnan	1992
Meghan Faughnan	1993
Susan Shepard	1994
Sue Shepard	1995
Meghan Faughnan	1996
Meghan Faughnan	1997
Emily Bohdan (tie)	1998
Kathleen Hamm (tie)	1998
Meghan Faughnan (tie)	1998
Meghan Faughnan	1999
Tiffany Giannandrea	2000
Andrea Bohdan	2001
Meghan Faughnan (tie)	2002
Christine Bragg (tie)	2002
Serra Akgun	2003
Christine Bragg	2004
Allison Hobbs	2005
Kelley King	2006
Morgan Tienken	2007

The 1969 Boys' Swimming Champion Dan Gerken is in lane 3.

Swimming pool.

Ann and Dick Gerken's aquatic children: Ann, Meg, and Dan.

Meg Gerken, girls' swimming champion in 1969.

Tennis Professionals

Clint Osborne 1957–1968
Don Leary 1968
Russ Harned
Rick Preston
Mike Geise 1978
Larry Openshaw 1979–1987
John Cleary 1988–1989
James McDonald 1990–1992
Patrick Kearns 1993–1994
Steve Hardin 1995–2003
Claes Westlin 2004–2005
Karl Levanat 2006–Present

Swim Coaches

Don Wilson 1957–1965
Charles Wenk .... 1966 (one half)
Don Karn .... 1966 (one half)–1968
Bob Grant 1969
Bob O'Connell 1970–1971
Don Wilson (returned for one year) 1972
Al Mulchay 1973
Mark Johnson 1974
Terry Sullivan 1975–1977
Bernie Rafferty 1978–1980
Ed Martin 1981
Skip DeNicola 1982–1985
Quentin Lawler 1986
Lisa O'Dell 1987
Bob Grant 1989
Maria Cornara Swami 1989
Bob Grant 1990
Pat Swift 1991–Present

NOTE: In 1989, Bob Grant and Maria Swami split the pool duties with Bob handling the swim team and Maria assuming the pool management responsibility.

Club Chefs

Emil (French)	1957	Mark Paolini (Italian)	1988–1990
Stefan (Alsace-Lorraine)	1957–1966	Bryan C. Previte (Italian)	1990–1998
Wolfgang Voss (German)	1966	Daniel Leviatin (Russian/Polish)	1998–2004
Konrad Renken (German)	1966–1989	J. B. Sipple, C.E.C.	2004–Present
Mazzocco (Italian)	1987*	*Konrad Renken returned to help.	

Executive Chef Konrad.

Chef Daniel Leviatin.

Chef Bryan C. Previte.

Chef J. B. Sipple.

Chronology

1957	Opening day, June 29
1958	Completed eighteen hole golf course
1959	Constructed ballroom, 19th Hole, and terrace
1960	Enlarged men's locker room, added flagstone to terrace, blacktopped driveway
1962	Added roof over terrace
1963	Altered lobby, relocated golf shop, contracted with Nutmeg Curling Club and built facility
1964	Relocated golf snack bar and paddle tennis courts
1965	Installed a fully automatic golf course irrigation system
1966	Added new dining room, mixed grill, and kitchen to clubhouse
1971	Added new men's grill and redecorated the ballroom
1973	Redesigned and rebuilt men's shower room
1975	Added two all weather tennis courts
1976	Added new golf course maintenance buildings
1979	Added new bathhouse, re-landscaped entire pool area, enlarged and winterized halfway house, and re-stored tennis shop
1982	Twenty-fifth anniversary year
1984	Added new 18th Green and enlarged practice areas
1986	Members purchased the club
1988	Redecorated the lobby, dining room, lounge, mixed grill, ballroom, and altered the entrance to the clubhouse
1990	Converted all weather tennis courts to Har-Tru, expanded tee on the 5th Hole, Phase I of the golf course drainage project completed
1991	Purchased and installed computer system and in-house laundry, Phase II of the golf course drainage project completed, converted from septic to sewer system
1992	Rebuilt the 9th and 16th tees, enlarged the 11th tee and the tennis shop, tiled snack bar deck at the pool, upgraded interior of the pool house
1993	Started and completed Phase I of the five year building renovation plan by rebuilding the back patio and changed the color of club buildings, completed Phase III of the golf course drainage project
1994	Started and completed Phase II of the five year building renovation plan by shingling pool house and curling building, re-roofing existing roofs and erecting new roof over the pool house and porte cochere, terraced back lawn area
1995	Rebuilt the 13th Hole with new tees; relocated the stream, new traps, mounds, and the course's first chipping area to the left of the green
1996	Complete renovation of the 13th Hole, enclosed and fenced a lawn area at the pool
1998	Renovations of club entrance on Mansfield Avenue.
1999	Renovated and gutted the main dining room, created a dome ceiling, renamed the room the Medallion Room
2000	Renovated the men's and women's locker rooms and lounges utilizing the curling rink once occupied by the Nutmeg Curling Club, removed the metal lockers and replaced them with modern wood lockers; a new meeting room was added on the second floor above the main kitchen, named and dedicated as the Auchincloss Room in honor of Edgar Auchincloss; removed the former ladies' locker room on the second floor above the main kitchen and replaced it with new accounting and management offices; "state of the art" exercise equipment was installed in the space above the satellite kitchen
2001	Renovated and reconfigured the main ballroom, lounge, and service bar including the addition of hardwood floors to the main hallway; upgraded the golf course irrigation system to a multi-row system; demolished the former men's locker room and shower to make room for the new satellite kitchen; added a new two-sided fieldstone fireplace to the pub with outside access by the terrace
2002	Expanded the size of the tee box on the golf course practice range
2003	Completed the new tennis center
2004	Upgraded the pool locker rooms and snack bar; replaced the clubhouse roof; renovated the mixed grill; created the new pub and terrace; expanded main irrigation pond
2007	Removed the telephone and utility lines and placed them underground; began the new pool and snack bar pavilion construction to be completed in spring of 2008; began the golf course renovation under the direction of golf course architect Dr. Michael J. Hurdzan.

Abercrombie, Abbott
Abood, John J.
Adam, Peter, J. C.
Adsit, Carl C.
Ahearn, Richard L.
Albert, Warren M.
Allen, Edwin C.
Allison, Charles F. P.
Altizer, Rimer Gaither
Auchincloss, Charles C.
Auchincloss, Mrs. Edgar S.
Auchincloss, S. S.

Bach, Julian Sebastian, Jr.
Baker, Alan E.
Baker, Davis L., Jr.
Baltz, William W.
Batten, Fred W.
Beagley, Bruce E., Jr.
Benedict, Raymond T.
Bescher, Orville Charles
Blackburn, Leonard A., Jr.
Bliss, Susan Dwight (Miss)
Boeckeler, Mary Hyde
   (Mrs. Henry A.)
Boyer, Pearce F., Jr.
Brameier, James W.
Brown, Darrell F.
Brown, Earl Al, Jr.
Brown, James M., Jr.
Bruce, Henry Eugene
Brunner, Albert L.
Bryant, John
Burleigh, Ernest H.
Burns, Edward H., Jr.

Cain, William E.
Callender, William H.
Calve, George M.
Calve, Joseph F.
Cannon, J. Thomas
Capstaff, Albert L.

Carroll, Dudley D., Jr.
Childs, Henry A.
Clark, Russell C., Jr.
Clarke, Francis A.
Clarke, John A.
Clewell, Dayton H.
Cochran, James J.
Cole, George Emerson
Collins, William F., II
Collins, William Howes
Conrade, Noel Lawrence,
   M.D.
Conhagen, Alfred
Connery, John Francis
Conetta, Louis D.
Corwin, Wallace G.
Coyle, Douglas Jay
Cullman, Lewis B.
Cutler, Benjamin C.

Davis, Ray F.
DeLeo, Samuel P.
Denning, James E.
DeVinne, Charles A.
Dick, George W.
DiGiacomo, Vincent
Dillon, Leonard A., Jr.
Dolian, Frank E.
Drowne, George P., Jr.
Drumm, Howard V.
Dudensing, Patrick L.
Dwyer, Gregory K.

Ellis, John
Emerson, Dow E.
Erdmann, Henry A. O.

Farnam, Frederick Z. B.
Farrell, John J.
Fedeler, John H. E.
Fellows, William Lee
Ferguson, John William II

Fine, William, M.
Finsthwait, Robert A.
Fitzpatrick, Arthur M.
Fladager, Vernon L.
Flynn, James W.
Fobes, Donald E.
Foote, George F., Jr.
Forkner, Dr. Claude E.
Forsdick, Charles Ernest
Forster, Norman D.
Fourton, Leslie Eugene
Friend, Alfred

Gaines, Robert W.
Gegenheimer, Harold W.
Geise, Edward J.
Getman, Kendall G.
Good, Thomas
Graves, Allan D.
Gregg, David, Jr.
Gregory, Paul
Groder, Linwood J.
Gwinner, Walter C.

Hackett, Joseph F.
Hackett, Walter J(oseph)
Haims, Walter R.
Hammond, Carleton E.
Hanish, Burton D.
Harris, James R., Jr.
Haskell, Sherwin T., Jr.
Hazelton, Benjamin F.
Herbert, John E.
Hergert, Harry H.
Hicks, William B.
Hilgeman, Edward Henry
Hill, Edward Lewis
Hines, Gordon H.
Holmes, William F.
Hopkins, Robert C.
Horn, William C.
Horton, Kingsley F.

Howell, H. Wardwell
Hufnagel, John A.
Hugo, Frederick V., Jr.
Hutchinson, William D.

Ingraham, Andrew C.
Ippolito, Vincent James
Irving, Michael Henry
Isaacson, Clifford

Jacobs, John III
Johannessen, John Eric
Johnson, Harold A., Jr.
Jones, Alexander, Jr.
Jones, John L., Jr.
Jones, Verner

Karl, James L.
Keefer, George
Kellam, John
Kerrigan, Thomas F.
Keyser, Gerald R.
King, Richard
King, William Lawrence
Kinlock, James F.
Knapp, George Owen
Kraig, Thomas L.
Kraus, Bernard J.

Ladue, James Warren
Langlie, Theos A.
Leach, Charles H.
Lehr, Walter
Leib, Samuel F.
Lewis, Robert E.
Lewis, Sherman Leland
Leuthold, Adolph
Lindenfelser, Richard
Lindgren, Vincent V.
Lindstrom, Arthur
Littlefield, Paul D.
Lovell, Gordon

Low, Stuart M.
Lundberg, Eric
Lydecker, Garrit A.

Macmillan, Hugh Frederick
Madden, Richard A.
Madsen, Edwin P.
Magrane, John K.
Mallory, William P.
Mandable, John E.
Mardfin, Robert K.
Matheson, Roderick, Jr.
McDonald, Samuel J.
McGarry, Richard J.
Melaugh, Owen H.
Meyer, Dr. and Mrs.
    Herbert H.
Mikolasy, William E.
Miller, Frank L. III
Milton, Charles A.
Moore, Edward Parsons
Moorman, Hiram Reginald
Morse, Edmond N.
Mygatt, Mrs. R. E.

Nagel, Allen P.
Ney, Edward N.
Nichols, Carl W., Jr.
Nordin, Anton B., Jr.
Norton, H. Ray

Oed, Edward W.
Orr, William T., Jr.

Page, Nelson L.
Palen, Cornelius
Paris, Donald M.

Parks, Charles O.
Penberthy, Philip E.
Petersen, Walter M.
Peterson, Morris
Petroccia, John A.
Pfeifer, Charles F.
Phelps, James F.
Pierpont, John H.
Plaut, Walter N.
Price, John W.
Primm, Robert T.

Raidt, Robert A.
Ralph, Dr. Fenn T.
Reback, Dan M.
Reed, Eugene Carroll
Reed, Robert J.
Reilly, Lawrence H., Jr.
Reiner, Laurence E.
Reinschild, Carl
Reis, Maurice J.
Rhody, Arthur R.
Rice, D. R.
Richardson, Thomas
    Murray
Rogers, J. Forbes, M.D.
Ross, Leroy
Rowland, Thomas F.
Rubino, John

Sachs, Walter Edward
Sandberg, Lars J.
Saunders, Kenneth W.
Scanley, Clyde S.
Schaffner, John L.
Schmidlein, Joseph A.
Schmidt, George A., Jr.

Schuyler, R(obert)
    T(enEyck)
Seaver, Howard E.
Seely, Holly H.
Seibert, Walter R.
Seipt, Richard
Selfridge, Charles F.
Sharpe, Leonard
    Worthington
Shaver, James Wilson
Simons, Langdon S., Jr.
Smith, Rollin C., Jr.
Smith, Royall G.
Smith, Warren I.
Soper, George A., Jr.
Stahman, Robert
Stark, Frank L., Jr.
Steele, David T. /
    Mrs. Nan C. Steele
Sterenberg, James W.
Stevens, Ambrose E.
Stevenson, Ward B.
Stewart, Thomas Oswald
Stonington, John E.
Stowe, David Beecher
Strauss, Henry
Stringer, Robert A.
Sulloway, Alvah W.

Tankoos, William G.
Taylor, Bruce L.
Taylor, Dale E.
Tiffany, Gordon M.
Tittmann, Eugene C., Jr.
Toumey, Hubert John
Townsend, Lee Dandridge
Travis, Charles M., Jr.

Tucker, William Randolph

Vail, Ben B.
Van Leight, Eugene J.
Van Loan, William Rodman
Verney, Ralph W.
Vickery, V(ictor) D(avis)
Vollmer, Arnold H.
Voris, Dr. Jacques Van
    Brunt

Wagner, Edward Lawrence
Walker, Dilworth H.
Wallace, Edward G.
Warner, Myron F.
Waters, Robert G.
Waters, Sanford
Watson, George W.
Weed, Clayton B., M.D.
West, John L.
Westerman, Jan H.
Weyeneth, Eugene E.
Wiesley, Donald Bruce
Wilkinson, Albert J.
Williams, Wilson M.
Wilson, Forbes Kingsbury
Wilson, James H.
Wilson, James Walton
Wilson, Ralph L.
Winans, Raymond P.
Winton, Clifford A.
Wright, David H.

Zangrillo, Peter Paul
Zangrillo, Steve

2007 Membership Roster

RG	Regular Golf
SR	Senior Golf
JG	Junior Golf
AG	Associate Golf
RT	Regular Tennis
TS	Tennis Senior
JT	Junior Tennis
JS	Junior Social Waiting Golf
SG	Social Waiting Golf
ST	Social Waiting Tennis
SS	Social Senior
SO	Social Other
NR	Non Resident

RG .... Abruzzese, Joseph (Sherri)
RG .... Adams, Wayne (Louella)
RT .... Akgun, Murat (Pamela)
RT .... Alfieri, Michael (Lisa)
RT ....Allen, Daniel (Stacie)
RG ....Alter, Barbara (John)
RT ....Amble, David (Joan)
RG .....Andrea, Anthony (Barbara)
SR. Annunziato, Dr. Lewis (Janet)
RG .... Anselmo, Frank (Christine)
NR .... Antin, Anthony (Jean)
RT ....Arnone, William (Patricia)
RG ....Atha, Stuart III (Janis)
RG ...Atkinson, Joseph (Kathleen)

NR .... Baetz, Ernest, Jr. (Gayle)
RG .... Baker, Charles (Lauren)
SO .... Ball, William (Mary Lou)
RG .... Balloch, Hugh (Susan)
RG .... Barna, John
RG .... Barton, David (Trisha)
RG ....Bay, Peter (Ellen)
RG .... Bayly, Daniel (Pamela)
SS .... Beagley, Bruce, Jr.
RT .... Becker, Jed (Elizabeth)
RT .... Begley, Robert (Barbara)
RG ....Bello, George (Carol)
RG ....Bello, Gregory
RG .... Bello, Mark
SS .... Benedict, Jean
RT ....Bennett, Richard G. (Mary Elizabeth)

SS ... Bennett, Richard M. (Dodie)
RG ...Berardino, Thomas (Charlene)
SG .... Bergen, Mark (Joan)
RT ....Bergmann, Oliver (Eileen)
RG ... Bieler, Andrew C. (Victoria)
NR .... Binks, Alastair (Kathy)
RG .... Binks, Malcolm (Jillian)
RG .... Bischoff, J. Michael (Rhea)
RG .... Bishko, Christopher
RG ....Bishko, John (Mary Ness)
RG ....Bishko, Michael (Carol)
RG..Blackman, John, Jr. (Kathleen)
NR....Blackwood, Adam (Michelle)
RT ...... Blatney, Stephen III (Cara)
RT .... Blaze, Clifford (Ana)
SS ....Bongiovanni, Nicholas
NR .... Bornhuetter, Cynthia
SR............. Bosch, Ralph (Edythe)
RT ....Bosek, James C. (Diane)
NR ....Bourne, Adrian (Gemma)
RG ....Bowes, John (Christine)
RG .... Bragg, James (Dee)
RG .... Bragg, Steven (Emily)
SO .....Brandon, Robert (Larraine)
RG ....Branigan, John D. (Jane)
RG ....Brewer, Hugh III (Karen)
NR ....Brier, Brendan
RG .... Brier, Timothy (Patricia)
RG .....Brindley, David (Margaret)
SR.......................Brindley, Velma
NR ....Brough, Graham (Sally)
NR .... Brown, James, Jr. (Anne)
RG .... Brunelle, John (Patricia)
RG .... Bryan, Lowell
RG ...Bulkin, Michael (Rosemary)
RG ..Buongiorno, Joseph (Rosina)
SO ....Busskohl, Terry (Barbara)
RG .... Byrne, Thomas (Peggy)

RG .... Calby, Douglas (Karen)
SR..............................Calve, Ann
RG ....Calve, Robert (Ann)
RG .....Calvillo, Ricardo (Markell)
RG ....Camilleri, Louis (Marjolyn)
SG ...Campbell, John W. (Debbie)
SO ....Caputo, Carl (Jeanne)
RG ....Carey, Douglas (Gene)
RG....Carty, James H. (Sarah Ellen)
RG ....Caruso, Victor (Jeannine)

RG ....Cassidy, Kevin (Jacqueline)
SS .... Castle, Richard (Burma)
SS .... Castle, Thomas (Judith)
RG .... Castrignano, Robert
RG .... Ceresa, Alfred (Susan)
RG .... Charles, John (Marsha)
RT .....Christopher, Thomas (Teresa)
RG ....Ciasullo, Paul (Marie)
RG .... Ciquera, Eleanor (James)
RG ....Clark, Brian G.
SR.............. Clay, T. Robert (Teri)
RG .... Cobb, Chester (Mary)
RG .... Coburn, Scott (Eileen)
RG ... Coleman, William (Patricia)
RG .... Coley, James (Deborah)
RG ....Conte, Rocco (Eileen)
NR ....Copeland, Jack
RG .... Corcoran, John (Wanda)
SO .... Corcoran, Kimberly
SS .... Cosgrove, Sheila
NR ....Coviello, Philip (Carole)
SR................... Cranston, George
RG .... Crawley, John B. (Ann)
RT .... Critelli, Michael (Joyce)
RT .... Crofton, Michael (Joan)
NR ....Crotty, Jeanne
SO ....Cudney, Richard L. (Tania)

RG.. D'Acunto, Dominick (Sharon)
RT ....D'Andrea, Ronald (Emily)
JG ... Davidson, Melissa (Thomas)
NR .... Davis, Baird (Patricia)
RT ....Davis, Peter (Susan)
RT .... Day, Jackson (Christian)
NR ....Deke, Daryl
RG .... Delaney, Michael (Maricel)
SG .... Dellarusso, Richard (Mary)
SS .... DelleFontane, Joseph
RG ....Deluca, Charles (Dawn)
NR .... Derbes, Richard (Kathleen)
RG ....DiBiasio, Adolf (Josephine)
JG ....DiBiasio, Daniel
JG .... DiBiasio, Michael
SG ...... Dickson, Duane (Barbara)
RT .... DiFazio, Frank (Maraja)
SS ....Dillon, Barbara
RT .... Dirvin, David (Constance)
RG .... Dister, Joseph (Jeanette)
RT .... Doherty, Christopher (Kelsey)

RG ..... Donoghue, Michael (Cece)
RG ... Dowling, Patrick (Kathleen)
RG..Duncan, Ian (Marjorie Anne)
RG ....Duncan, Neil (Kara-Ellyn)
JG .... Dunlap, Alyson (Dirk)
RG .... Dunlop, Henry (Dana)

SG ....Ekern, Nigel P.
RG ....Ely, James (Elisabeth)
RG ....Eppley, S. Kent (Lisa)
RG ....Epstein, Jeffrey (Sue)
SR.........Erikson, Walter (Bernice)
RG ....Esposito, Mark (Gina)
RG .... Ettinger, Richard (Joan)
RG .... Evanson, Paul (Carol)

SR....... Fager, Donald (Geraldine)
RG .... Falco, Neil (Christine)
RG .... Faughnan, Kevin (Peggy)
NR .... Ferm, David (Molly)
RG ....Ferm, David, Jr. (Laura)
JG .... Ferm, John (Jennifer)
RG ..... Ferrante, Victor (Margaret)
SG .... Feuerman, Kurt (Anne)
RG .... Filatov, Geri
NR ....Fischer, John (Carolyn)
RT ...... Fitzpatrick, Steven (Laura)
RG .... Flanagan, Lawrence (Stephanie)
RG .... Flynn, Robert (Roseanne)
RT ...... Foley, Robert III (Barbara)
RT .... Forkner, Stanley (Wendy)
RG ....Fowler, Frank (Susan)
RT ....Fox, Mark (Tracy)
SG ....Frazier, William
RG ....Friend, Warren (Holly)
RG .... Friese, Newton (Dede)

SG ....Gabriele, Neil
RG ...... Gagliardi, Michael (Lynn)
RG .... Gardner, Robert (Beth)
RG ....Gartin, Clint (Karen)
RT ....Gartland, William (Michele)
RG ......Gatewood, Gary (Barbara)
RG .....Gebbia, Charles (Kathleen)
RT ....Genco, William (Mary)
RG ..... Giannos, Dennis (Marilyn)
SR....... Giegerich, Lester (Lillian)
RG .... Gifford, Benjamin (Jane)

RG .... Gilliam, George (Diane)
NR .. Goldberg, Keith (Leigh Ann)
SS .... Goodall, John (Patricia)
JG .... Gorman, Christopher
NR .... Gorman, Donald (Valerie)
NR .... Gould, John (Caroline)
SS .... Gould, Margaret
RG .... Grant, John III (Nancy)
RG .... Green, Robert S. (Tami)
RG .... Green, Stephen M.
RG .... Greene, Alan (Brenda)
RG ..... Greenspon, Robert (Claire)
RG .... Griffin, John (Mary)
RT .... Grune, Steven B. (Nancy)
JT .... Grunow, Dana (Ben)
RG ...... Gruppo, Stephen (Allison)
SG ..... Gummenson, Peter (Susan)

JG .... Hahn, Adam
RG .... Hahn, James (Stephanie)
NR .... Hahn, James, Jr. (Tawn)
NR .... Haines, Michael (Joanne)
RT .... Halloran, Todd (Julie)
RG ..... Halsey, William A. (Carolyn)
RG Halvorsen, Ole Andreas (Diane)
JG .... Hanford, James
RG .... Hanford, Maurice III (Eileen)
RT .... Hardison, Joseph H. III
(De Ann)
RG .... Hargrove, Thomas
SS .. Harrington, Jerome (Barbara)
RG ..... Harter, Richard (Catherine)
RG .... Hayes, Michael
RG .... Hayes, William (Gloria)
RG .... Healy, Patrick (Julie)
SG ... Heaney, Christopher (Heidi)
RG .... Heineman, Benjamin
(Christine)
RT .... Helgans, David (Letty)
RT .... Helms, Theodore (Susan)
RG .... Hendrickson, David
RG .... Hendrickson, Paul (Joan)
RT .... Henn, Joseph (Marie)
SG .... Hennessy, Paul (Joanne)
RG .. Herbert, John, Jr. (Lyn Nevins)
SR .... Herbert, Kathleen
RG .... Herdman, Robert (Marikay)
RG ....Heuer, Alan (Jean)
JG .... Hickey, Alison (Gregory)
RG .... Higgins, John (Barbara)
SS .... Hindenach, Lee (Dorothy)
RG .... Hires, R. Byard (Anne)
RG ...... Hobbs, Steven (Elizabeth)
RG .... Hogan, Alan (Catherine)
RG .... Holland, Susan
(Christopher)

RG .... Holligan, Pamela
JG .... Holligan, William
RG .... Holloway, Gary (Julie)
SR .... Holmer, Edwin (Mary)
SS .... Holt, Bonnie
RG .... Holub, Roland (Patricia)
RG .... Horoszko, Peter (Iana)
RG .... Howell, Jeanne
RG ... Hughes, Dr. Robert (Alison)
RG .... Hughes, Tamara Hanford
(Daniel)
SS .... Hulsey, Betsy
NR .... Huntington, Earl (Phyllis)
JG .... Hurst, Carolyn (Anders)
RG ... Hutchins, Lawrence (Peggy)

JG ... Imbrogno, Michael (Christine)
RG .... Imbrogno, Peter (Margaret)
SS .... Irwin, John (Elizabeth)

RG .... Jaeger, Carl (Helen)
JG ... Jandovitz, Jocelyn (Thomas)
RT .... Jennings, William (Cheri)
RG .... Jessiman, Alistair (Laura)
RG .... Jester, William (Donna)
JG ..... Johnson, Kristin (Christian)
RG ..... Johnson, Sheldon (Peachy)
RG .... Jones, Frank (Gail)
RG .... Joyce, Thomas (Lisa)
RG .... Juterbock, Thomas

RG .... Kamford, Daria
RG .... Kaye, Ronald (Sue Ellen)
RG .... Keane, John (Mary)
RG .... Keating, Kevin (Nancy)
RG .. Keating, Kevin, Jr. (Jennifer)
SO .... Kelly, Ann (Joseph)
RT .... Kelly, David (Caryn)
RG .... Kelly, Peter (Barbara)
RT .... Kelly, Thomas (Claire)
RG ...... Kelly, Timothy (Christine)
RT .... Kennedy, Morgan (Jennifer)
RG .... Kensington, Costa (Cheryl)
NR .... Kimball, Paul (Kathleen)
RG .... King, John, Jr. (Margery)
NR .... Kinney, Robert (Merilee)
ST .... Kirby, Drew (Sally)
RG ..... Kosnik, Richard (B. Leigh)
SG .... Kulak, Kevin (Erin)

SR .... LaBanca, Alfred (Joan)
SR .... LaForte, Dr. Peter (Jeannette)
RG .... LaMantia, Kimberly
SR .... Land, Gay (Elizabeth)
RT .... Lane, Alexander (Elizabeth)
RG .... Laracy, M. A. (Sue Ellen)

SO .... Larson, Paul S. (Molly)
RT .... LaVecchia, Pat (Kris)
RG .... Lavery, John (Kathryn)
RG .... Lawrence, Edward, Jr.
(Deborah)
RG .... Lay, Donald (Mary)
RG .... Leach, Wilson (Jackie)
RT .. Leclerc, Real Henri-Paul (Tara)
RG .... Lee, Robert (Debi)
RG .... Lincoln, Robert (Sheryl)
JG .... Lodge, Andrew (Cari)
AG .... Lodge, Gigi
RG .... Lom, Thomas (Winifred)
RG .... Long, James A. (Susan)
ST .... Loomis, Stillman (Ellen)
SG ..... Lopiano, Steven (Caroline)
RG .... Lorelli, Michael (Nancy)
NR. Lougee, Virginius B. (Dorothy)
RG .... Love, Jane
NR .... Love, Richard (Margaret)
NR ... Lovejoy, Robert, Jr. (Becky)
SS ... Lundberg, C. Eric (Joan)
RG .. Lundberg, Theodore (Nancy)
RG ... Luttrell, John (Thelma May)
RT .... Luttrell, Steven (Michelle)
RG .... Lyle, Robert S. (Barbara)
RG ... Lynch, Albert, Jr. (Bernadette)
RG .... Lynch, David (Evelyn)
RG .... Lyons, Edward, Jr. (Jane)
NR .... Lyons, Frank
RG .... Lyons, Michael (Emily)

RT ..... Maccarone, Justin, Jr. (Marie)
RG .... Mahoney, Daniel (Kristine)
SG .... Major, David (Kimberly)
RG .... Mallozzi, Robert (Phyllis)
RT .... Marcantonio, Cheryl
SO .... Marr, John (Karen)
RG .... Marsh, Robert (Celeste)
NR ...... Martin, Donald (Cathleen)
NR ...... Martin, Stephen (Danielle)
RG ... Martorella, Rebecca (Richard)
RG ... Massamillo, Eugene (Susan)
NR ... Massie, Adrian, Jr. (Eleanor)
RG .... Matheis, Michael (Dana)
SO .... Mathews, Warren (Gail)
RG ... Matsuzaka, Yoichi (Sayoko)
RG ... Matthews, Douglas (Nancy)
RT .... Mauboussin, Michael
(Michelle)
RG .... May, David (Katrina)
RG .... Mayo, J. Robb (Susan)
JG .... Mayo, R. Scott
RG ... McAllister, Dennis (Deidre)
RT .... McCabe, James III (Christine)
NR ..... McCann, David (Margaret)

SG .... McCarthy, Taryn (Greer)
RG .. McClutchy, John H., Jr. (Janet)
JG .... McClutchy, Todd
SO .... McCormick, Peter (Jean)
RG ..... McDonald, Kevin (Ginger)
RG ... McDonough, Patrick (Nella)
RG .... McGrath, Mark
RG ..... McGrath, Thomas (Laurie)
RG ..... McGroarty, Robert (Betsy)
NR .... McKeon, Paul (Nanette)
RG ... McKeown, Kerry (William)
RG .... McKiernan, Christopher
(Terri)
RG ...... McKiernan, Kevin (Kerry)
JG .... McKiernan, Patrick
RG ... McKiernan, Thomas (Terry)
RG .... McLaughlin, Edwin, Jr.
(Barbara)
RG .... McLaughlin, Nancy
NR .... McManus, Edward (Barbara)
RG .... McManus, Edward, Jr.
RT .... McNulty, Daniel
RG .... McQuilkin, Kevin (Debbie)
SR .... Meagher, James (Harriet)
RG .... Meck, Todd (Susanne)
RG .... Meier, Robert (Elizabeth)
SG .... Melz, Stephen (Donna)
NR .... Mende, Hans (Maria)
RG ...... Metzger, James (Belinda)
RG .... Metzger, Peter (Inga)
NR .... Meyer, Michael (Katy)
RG ...... Millard, James (Kathleen)
RG .. Milunovich, Steven (Pamela)
ST ..... Misthopoulos, Tricia (Noel)
RG .. Mobyed, Robert (Mary Jean)
SG .... Moley, Peter (Elizabeth)
SG .... Molloy, Ross (Kimberly)
NR ... Montero, Alfredo (Lorraine)
RG ....Moore, Thomas (Erma)
RG .... Moore, Willett S., Jr. (Lois)
SS .... Mullen, Gloria
RG. Mulligan, William, Jr. (Wendy)
RG .... Munro, Douglas (Becky)
RG .... Murphy, James (Sandra)
RG .... Murphy, Nikki
RG .... Murphy, Peter (Toni)
RG ..... Musicaro, John, Jr. (Diane)
SS .... Muth, Isabelle

RT .... Nackley, David (Heather)
SG .... Naughton, Kevin (Heidi)
RG .... Nava, Eloy L. (Diane)
RG .... Nelson, Peter (Deborah)
SG .... Nemec, David (Kristin)
RG .... Newton, Russell (Kelly)
RG .... Nicholls, Edward (Stacie)

SG .... Nicoletti, Peter (Joan)
RG .... Nielsen, Joanne
RT .... Nolte, Reed (Leslie)
RG .... Noschese, Victor (Laura)
RG ... Noujaim, Alexander (Diane)
RG .... Noujaim, Fares (Mirna)
RG .... Nugent, Kevin (Teri)
NR ..... Nutting, William (Jennifer)

RG .... Obernier, Robert (Rosemarie)
RG .... Oca, Robert (Christine)
NR ...... O'Kelley, Ronald (Lesley)
SG .... Olsen, John (Rosanne)
NR .... Olsen, Warren (Guerin)
SS .... O'Neill, Patrick (Sandra)
RG .... O'Rourke, Brendan

RG .... Palmer, Alphonse (Patsy)
RT ...... Palmer, Gregory (Susanne)
RT .... Palmer, Steven (Laura)
RG .... Pankosky, Jay (Jill)
SS .... Parker, James (Helen)
JG .... Passaro, Christopher
RG .... Patrone, Enrico (Marie)
RG .... Peck, Nathan, Jr. (Robin)
NR .... Peeling, John (Donna)
RG ...... Peglar, Robert (Mary Ann)
RG .... Pelli, Frank (Anita)
RG .... Peppet, Russell (Sandra)
RG .... Perry, Matthew (Karen)
NR .... Peters, Philip, Jr. (Tamie)
RG .... Phillips, Craig (Liz)
RG .... Piantidosi, Frank (Florence)
RG .. Piccaro, Dr. Christopher (Tina)
SR .... Pierson, Stephen (Nancy)
RG .... Polett, David E. (Karen)
RG .... Powell, Craig (Marie)
RG .... Powell, Michael (Nancy)
RG .... Price, John (Liz)
JT .... Prichard, Pamela (Duncan)
SS .... Primm, Gerry
NR .... Princi, Anthony (Cynthia)
SG .... Pryor, Martin (Megan)
RT .... Pugh, Walter (Sybil)
RG .... Purcell, Ann S.

RG .... Qua, John (Suzanne)

SO .... Raver, William (Sarah)
RT .... Rech, Dolly
RG .... Rehlaender, James (Janis)
RG .... Reilly, John (Ann Marie)
SS .... Reilly, Lawrence, Jr.
(Katherine)
NR .... Reiss, Paul (Lisa)
SO .... Riggio, Roy (Barbara)

RT .... Rintoul, Michael S. (Lisa)
RG .... Rischman, Douglas
(Kathleen)
RG .... Roach, Stephen S. (Katie)
RG .... Roberto, A. Robert
(Rosemary)
SR .... Robinson, Clark (Bea)
RG .... Robustelli, Richard (Kathy)
SG .... Roche, William (Lisa)
RG .... Rogers, James (Shirley)
RG .... Rogers, Peter (Kathleen)
RG .... Romano, Douglas
RG .... Romano, Rita
RG .... Romanos, Jack (Mary)
RT .... Ropp, Willson (Margaret)
RG .... Ross, Marty (Elizabeth)
RG .... Rosser, Harold (Rita)
RG ..... Russell, Robert K. (Susan)
JG .... Russell, Robert K., Jr.
NR .... Ryan, John M. (Sheelagh)
RG .... Ryan, Michael (Diane)
RG .... Ryan, Thomas (Justine)

SG ..... Salvatore, Ronald (Joanne)
SS .... San Fan Andre, Marjorie
RG .... Santella, Peter (Regina)
SO .... Santos-Buch, Sharon
SS .... Santosus, Carol Ann
SG .... Sarbinowski, Joseph (Amy)
RG ..... Saverine, Robert (Barbara)
RG ..... Scala, A. Richard (Patricia)
RT .... Schloss, Edwin (Maureen)
NR .... Schmalzried, Marvin
RG .. Schmidt-Fellner, Peter (Diane)
RG ...... Scholl, W. Brooks (Robin)
RG .... Sclafani, Chip (Suzy)
SR .... Scott, Tucker M. Jr.
SS .... Seely, Estelle
RG .... Shea, Dennis (Kathy)
NR .. Shepard, William B. (Midge)
RG .. Shergalis, Edward (Dorothy)
SO .... Sherwood, Ann
RT .... Sherwood, David C. (Rhonda)
RT .... Shindler, Steven (Mary)
RG .... Siciliano, Peter (Rebecca)
RT ...... Sinacore, Stephen (Lauren)
SG .... Slapnicka, Tim (Carolyn)
JG .... Slattery, Holly (John)
ST .... Slotkin, Todd (Judy)
RG .... Smego, Dr. Douglas
(Mary Ann)
RG .. Smith, Bernard L. Jr. (Sonia)
SG .... Smith, Brian (Amanda)
RG .... Smith, Mark (Vicki)
RT .... Smith, Robert (Barbara)
RG ...... Smith, Shapleigh (Joanne)

RG .... Smoltz, Joseph (Marie)
RG ... Smoltz, Kenneth (Elizabeth)
RG .... Snyder, Christopher (Anne)
RG .... Solazzo, Steven (June)
RG .... Sommer, Gordon (Jennifer)
SS .... Sonnekson, Claire
JT .... Spataro, Lauren (James)
RG .... Speranza, William
(Betty Ballinger)
RG .... Spillane, Paul, Jr. (Hope)
RG .... Srader, Ronald (Jayne)
RT .. Stack, Christopher (Cathleen)
SO ...... Stanley, James, Jr. (Judith)
RG .... Steiner, Ernest (Anna)
RG .... Stelben, Robert (Maryanne)
JG .... Stelben, Robert, Jr.
RG .... Stevenson, John (Jayme)
RT .... Stewart, Christian (Cindy)
SG .... Stewart, Richard (Kelly)
SS ..... Stewart, Willard (Christine)
RG .... Stoetzer, John (Nancy)
SR .... St. Onge, Ronald J.
RT .... Stout, Christopher (Lisa)
RG .... Straus, John A. (Diane)
SO ...... Stuart, Lennox (Marjorie)
G .... Stuek, William (Laurie)
RT .... Stute, Jeffrey A. (Jill)
RG .... Sweeney, Edward, Jr.
(Catherine)

SG .... Tavlarios, John (Linda)
RG .... Taylor, Dennis (Carol)
RG .... Taylor, Lou (Tammy)
SG ..... Thornbury, Jeffrey (Leslie)
SS .... Thorne, Harriette
RT .... Tienken, Janine (Douglas)
SO .... Tobin, Frederick (Carroll)
RG .... Tobin, James (Karen)
JG .... Tonkovich, David
RG . Tonkovich, Eugene (Elfriede)
RG .... Topper, Bernard
(Maureen Ann)
RG .... Torey, Donald (Jennifer)
ST ..... Tortorella, Michael (Nancy)
SS .... Toumey, Dorothy
RG .... Tracy, Joseph (Ellen)
RT .... Trask, Edward (Laura)
RG .... Traver, Douglas (Jean)
RG .... True, R. Stephen (Elaine)
SG .... Tuccio, Edward (Kimberly)
RG ... Tuzinkiewicz, Paul (Kristin)

RG .... Vanacore, Mark (Tricia)
RG . Van Keuren, Robert (Deirdre)
NR ...... Vascellaro, Jerome (Mary)
RG .... Vasily, John (Medina)

NR .... Velie, Dianalee
SO ... Verhaegen, Dennis (Cecelia)
RT .... Vogel, Roger (Susan)
RG .... Voigt, Paul (Lilian)
RG Von Oehsen, David T. (Cathy)
RG .... Vossler, Michael (Heidi)

RT .... Waldron, Kevin (Lauri)
RG .... Walsh, Kevin (Kathleen)
RG .... Walsh, Peter (Rachel)
RT .. Wappler, William (Catherine)
SG .... Warnock, Robert (Amy)
SS .... Warr, Jane
RT .... Watson, Brian (Patricia)
NR .... Watson, Kelly (John)
NR .... Watson, Richard
RT .. Weatherstone, Dennis (Marion)
RG .... Weaver, Paul (Kathy)
RG .... Weiner-Trapness, Helge
(Carolyn)
NR .... Wellman, Michael (Lynn)
RG ...... Wells, Douglas (Nancy)
SR ...... Wenger, David (Yvette)
SS .... Wenger, Virgil (Jo)
SO .... Whaley, William (Nancy)
RG .... White, Clyde (Carter)
RT .... White, Richard (Virginia)
SR .... White, Thomas (Tecla)
RG .... Wilcock, Thomas (Laura)
RG .... Willett, Edward (Susan)
RG ..... Williams, Paul (Mary Lou)
SO .... Williams, Virginia
SS ... Wilson, Charles (Frances)
RG .... Winebrenner, David
(Elizabeth)
RG ...... Winter, Schuyler (Patricia)
RG .... Wisinski, Guy (Pam)
RG .... Wolcott, John (Jane)
RG .... Woodberry, Sturgis
(Carolyn)
SR ..... Wright, Philip (Anne Ernst)
RG ..... Wright, Steven A. (Alison)
NR .... Wulff, John (Linda)
RG .... Wyndorf, Gerald (Julie)

NR .... Youle, Jeffrey (Catherine)
RG .... Yowan, David (Cynthia)

RG .... Zaffino, Peter (Kirsten)
RT .... Zamsky, Steven (Maeve)
RG .... Zangrillo, Anthony
RG .... Zangrillo, Gina
SR ... Zangrillo, Stephen (Yolanda)
RG .... Zeko, Fehmi (Mary)
RG ..... Zinkand, Dennis (Suzanne)

About the Authors

Robert Lockwood Mills spent most of his adult life as a broker with Wall Street firms. But even while managing investment portfolios for his clients, he found time to indulge two other passions, writing and historical research.

In 1994 Mills authored his first book, *It Didn't Happen the Way You Think* (Heritage Books), a revisionist account of the Lincoln assassination. In 1999 his docudrama on the same topic, *The Trial of John Wilkes Booth*, was broadcast on Connecticut Public Radio. After retiring from his "day job" in 2001, Mills produced *The Last Renaissance Man* (Rutledge Books), a biography of CCD member Charles H. Mullen; co-authored *The Illustrated History of Stamford* (CT) for American Historical Press; and co-authored *The Man Who Kept the Secret*, a biography of PepsiCo executive Thomas Elmezzi. In 2005 his book *The Lindbergh Syndrome: Heroes and Celebrities in a New Gilded Age* (Fenestra Books), he describes the cultural milieu surrounding the 1927 trans-Atlantic flight of long-time Darien resident Charles A. Lindbergh.

Robert Lockwood Mills also edited five *Reader's Digest Illustrated Trade Books* on historical topics. A veteran actor, he wrote and directed four plays for the Darien Arts Council. He writes song lyrics and constructs crossword puzzles, and most recently completed work on *Baseball—Then and Now*, a nostalgic trip through the history of the Great American Pastime, due for release in 2009. Mills is a widower with three grown daughters and four grandchildren. He lives in Sun City Center, Florida.

Tucker Scott was born on the Eastern Shore of Virginia and educated at Randolph Macon College. He served in the U.S. Navy as a lieutenant senior grade communications officer in the South Pacific during World War II. He witnessed from his ship, the *Lavaca*, the signing of the peace treaty with the Japanese by General Douglas MacArthur aboard the *Battleship Missouri* while anchored in Tokyo Bay on September 2, 1945. After the war, he pursued a long career in broadcasting, starting as a trainee with the Compton Advertising Company. He moved on to Batten, Barton, Durstine and Osborn where he established the first media department in the advertising industry that was exclusively dedicated to the relatively new television technology. There he introduced eighty-two advertisers to the new TV medium. After growing that department from three people to thirty-seven in five years, he moved on to join John Blair Company where he became vice president of sales of their radio division. He retired in 1973.

Tucker was married to the late Melissa Mason for fifty-eight years and had three children. He has been a member of the Country Club of Darien since 1958 and served on the board of directors in the 1970s and 1980s. He served as the chairman of the James McGuire Caddie Fund for eleven years and was the liaison for the Nutmeg Curling Club. He now resides in New Canaan, Connecticut, and looks forward to playing the closing scrambles each year at CCD.